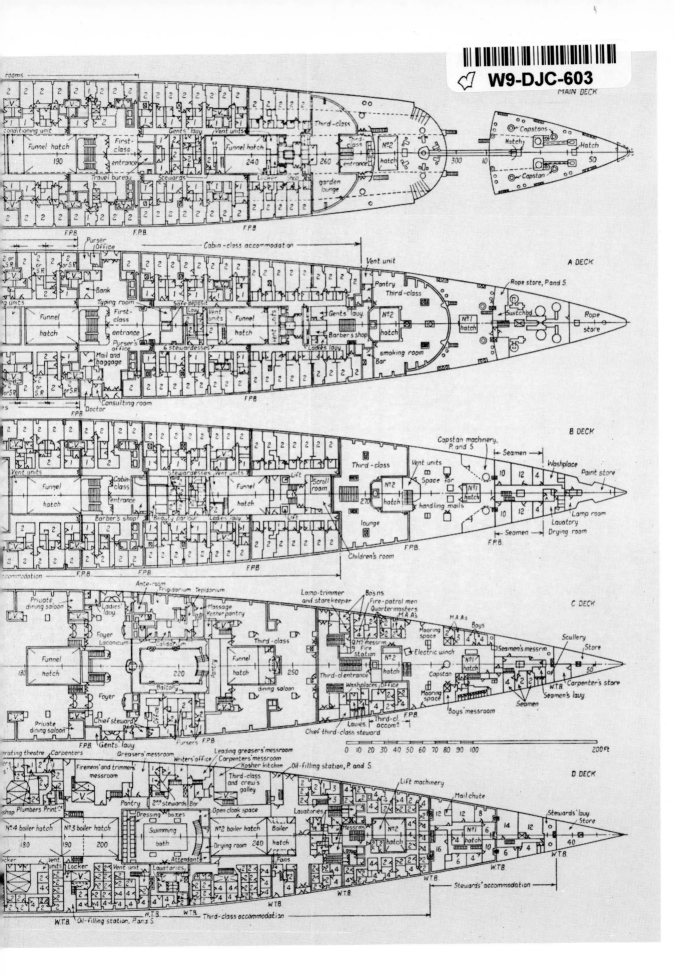

The
QUEEN MARY

—— *Her early years recalled* ——

The
QUEEN MARY

Her early years recalled

C.W.R. WINTER

W · W · Norton & Company

NEW YORK   LONDON

First American edition 1986

First published 1986

British Library Cataloguing in Publication Data

Winter, C. W. R.
The Queen Mary: her early years recalled.
1. Queen Mary (*Ship*)———History
I. Title
387.2'432   VM383.Q4

ISBN 0-393-02351-6

W. W. Norton & Company, Inc.,
500 Fifth Avenue, New York, New York 10110.
W. W. Norton & Company, Ltd.,
37 Great Russell Street, London, WC1B 3NU.

Printed in Great Britain

1 2 3 4 5 6 7 8 9 0

Contents

The Queen Mary: vital statistics

Builders
Messrs John Brown & Company Ltd, Clyde-bank.

Launch
26 September 1934, by Her Majesty Queen Mary, who was accompanied by His Majesty King George V, and the Prince of Wales (later King Edward VIII).

Departure from Clydebank
24 March 1936.

Maiden voyage
27 May 1936. (Southampton-Cherbourg-New York.)

Tonnage
80,773 tons gross.

Dimensions
Length overall 1,018 ft; on waterline, 1,004 ft. Beam 118 ft. Height—keel to top superstructure, 135 ft; keel to top forward funnel, 180 ft; keel to masthead, 234 ft.

Design
Over 8,000 experiments on numerous models in an experimental tank were conducted before the form of the great vessel was finally determined, in the course of which some 22 models travelled a total distance of over 1,000 miles up and down the tank.

Rivets
Riveting operations involved the use of over 10,000,000 rivets which if placed end to end would stretch a distance of over 270 miles.

Windows
The *Queen Mary* has about 2,000 portholes and windows. The area of glass is more than 2,500 sq ft. The panes of glass range from those one foot in diameter to large oval panes over two feet in height.

Stern frame and rudder
The total weight of the stern frame shaft brackets and rudder is nearly 600 tons.

Prologue

The 'Boat Train' pulls slowly into its special platform alongside the Ocean Dock, and disgorges its load of excited passengers. For many travellers from England the journey to New York has already begun in London, at Waterloo Station, from whence the '*Queen Mary* Special' has carried them swiftly and effortlessly to within a few yards of the ship that is to take them across the Atlantic. As they spill out on to the platform, clutching their hand luggage, the thought uppermost in every mind is to obtain their first glimpse of the *Queen Mary* about which they have read and heard so much.

The effect of this moment is invariably the same, a sudden though temporary pause in the excited chatter as the huge bulk of the ship comes into view. The *Queen Mary* dominates her surroundings. She towers over the large transit sheds and dwarfs the many dockside cranes, she reduces the railway lines and rolling stock to Lilliputian proportions. Not only the height of her black painted hull and white superstructure, but its length also, quite takes the breath away. It seems impossible to believe that such an enormous structure is actually afloat and is capable of moving at high speed through the water.

As passengers hurry towards the ship the bustle and excitement of the quay increases. Stewards dressed in their new *Queen Mary* uniforms trundle large trolleys loaded with piles of expensive-looking luggage towards the ship, each suitcase and trunk proudly displaying special *Queen Mary* labels bearing a picture of the ship, and giving information as to the owner's identity, cabin number, deck and class.

There are several covered gangways sloping gently up from the quay to shipside doors, their white canvas sides proclaiming the hardly necessary information that this is indeed the RMS *Queen Mary*. Footsteps automatically quicken as these gangways come into view. Pursers in smart uniforms stand at the foot of the gangways, smiling a welcome and checking tickets. At the top of the drugget carpeted, canvas-covered tunnels a further welcome awaits.

Here you step into a different world, a new world. A world of luxury, of friendly service, in which for the next four and a half days everything will be provided, and your only thought will be to enjoy yourself. Your immediate surroundings are panelled in fine woods, close carpeted and brilliantly lit, a foyer of which any luxury hotel would be proud. Helpful and friendly officials direct you to the lifts which will take you to your stateroom, stewards relieve you of the need to carry anything, and already you begin to get the feeling that you are the most important passenger Cunard has ever had the pleasure of serving.

Inside the ship all is calm, save for the excited conversation of fellow passengers. Your cabin steward is waiting to welcome you, to show you your stateroom and answer questions—sailing time, lunch arrangements, etc, etc. The decor of the cabin holds your attention for a moment, and then the sophistication of the bathroom too. Every cabin in this part of the ship is different, each one designed by an artist in interior decoration, each one having its own character.

Out on deck the general excitement is mounting as passengers explore the ship, discovering new delights. Last minute conversations are being held with friends who will shortly have to leave and return to their humdrum lives ashore. On the Sun Deck the rail is lined with people looking down nearly a hundred feet to the quay below where preparations are being made for departure, some of the baggage gangways having already been removed.

Finally, over the loudspeakers comes the awaited message—'All ashore who are going ashore!' and a thrill of excitement passes through every passenger. The voyage is about to begin.

Acknowledgements

I would like to express my thanks to the following individuals, all of whom have been helpful in obtaining illustrations for this book: Mr Jim Wilson, director of Govan Shipbuilders Ltd; Miss Andrea Rudd, Liverpool University Archives; Mrs Alma Topen, Glasgow University Archives; Mr Ray Sprake, chairman, Isle of Wight branch of the World Ship Society.

Chapter 1

A landsman goes to sea

My first glimpse of the Queen Mary was on a foggy morning early in January 1936. She was lying in the fitting out basin of John Brown's Clydebank Yard, and certainly dwarfed the buildings surrounding her. I had expected to see a very large ship, and I was not disappointed. She looked huge. As this is a personal account of the years I subsequently spent as a member of her crew, perhaps I may be forgiven for explaining how it was I came to be there at all.

After four years in the Engineering Department of University College, Nottingham, I had graduated as an electrical engineer, and had gone to work as a college apprentice with The British Thomson Houston Co Ltd. In those days opportunities for graduate electrical engineers were virtually limited to two firms, BTH of Rugby, and Metropolitan Vickers of Manchester. Both firms ran a five-year apprenticeship scheme for graduates, and paid during this period a wage of 47 shillings per week, less the usual stoppages. The scheme assured them a steady flow of (theoretically) trained engineers for their test bed, but many of the apprentices felt that the wage was hardly adequate, and that they were not getting a fair crack of the whip.

When the time came for me to take up my appointment with BTH, the company switched me from the main works at Rugby to their electric motor factory in Blackheath, near Birmingham. In doing so they explained that this was only a temporary measure for three months, and that at the end of this period I would return to Rugby and start my five-year tour of the various manufacturing departments. At the end of this tour they dangled, as bait, the possibility of a steady job with them at £250 per annum.

The conditions in the Blackheath factory were pretty grim, the test bed was positively dangerous, and the experience gained was of limited value. After six months therefore, with no sign of a transfer to Rugby, I wrote to the personnel manager, with whom I thought I had established a pleasant, friendly relationship. His reply was terse, and pointed out that I was a very small cog in a very large machine, and that they would move me when and if they felt fit. This I regarded as the ultimate straw, and began to look round for ways of escape.

At this time the publicity for the *Queen Mary*, the new wonder ship, was tremendous, and was hotting up to an enormous climax aimed to coincide with her maiden voyage the following May. Her history to date had been eventful and not entirely happy, for during the depression of the early 1930s all work on her had been stopped, and for some considerable time she had lain on the ways, slowly rusting to death. So that when, thanks to government help, work was resumed it became doubly important to bring her building to a successful conclusion. Hence, a publicity campaign was mounted, and this ultimately had the whole nation by the throat.

More in hope than in anger therefore I wrote to Cunard White Star, briefly explaining my background and training, and asking if they could find me a job in the ship. Their reply was discouraging. They sent me a form to fill in, and on reading it my heart sank. Practically all the questions they asked concerned the ships previously served in, with details of boiler capacity, type of equipment used, etc, and as I remember it now the completed form consisted mainly of my name and address at the top, a signature at the bottom, and a series of dashes in between.

Having posted it off to Liverpool I promptly

forgot about it and started to search elsewhere. But three weeks later, on a Wednesday morning, a telegram arrived saying; 'Report this office Friday for interview. Letter following. Signed, Cunard-Star.' No word of the *Queen Mary*, nor any other explanation.

Not knowing what the reaction of the factory manager would be to a request for a day off for the interview I decided to tell him about it afterwards, and on Friday I did not present myself for work. As I was eating my bacon and egg at breakfast—my landlady was an excellent cook—the postman arrived with the letter from Cunard. This confirmed that the interview was for a vacancy which had occurred in the engine room of the *Queen Mary*, and as I read these magic and exciting words my stomach turned over, and my breakfast remained unfinished.

In due course I presented myself at the awe-inspiring Cunard building in Liverpool and found the right office. I knocked at the window and announced my arrival. A man with a handful of papers came out to see me, and after shaking hands said 'You will be seeing the doctor at four o'clock, and there are several papers for you to sign. Here is your railway warrant to Glasgow, you will travel up tomorrow morning, and join the ship in the afternoon.'

He paused and saw the look of blank astonishment on my face.

'You are going to take this job, aren't you?' he said.

'I really don't know' I replied, 'I've still got a job in Blackheath, and they don't even know that I've come for the interview!'

He laughed. 'Well, in that case' he said, 'I'd better tell you a bit more about it, and leave you to think it over.'

And so he told me. The job was that of a Junior Sea-going Electrician in the *Queen Mary*. The money was £9 per month, plus keep, and when in service there would be one trip off per annum. Officers' accommodation in the ship was to Tourist Class standard, but the officers' mess room was served from the First Class (Cabin) Galley. One servant was provided to look after two officers, and there were other fringe benefits, such as an issue of fresh fruit every day. While in Glasgow there would be an additional subsistence allowance of £6 per week. And with that he left me, saying he would be back in ten minutes.

These ten minutes were the shortest yet most harrowing of my life. Up to this moment my career as an engineer had been predictable and conventional, and here I was being presented with the opportunity of throwing it all to the winds and making a violent change in direction. It was a horrible decision to have to take, and there was no-one I could consult. My parents were in Nottingham, my fiancée was in Norfolk, and the minutes were ticking away. The wages sounded poor, but it must be remembered that this was 1936, when money was much more like money. The living conditions certainly sounded reasonable.

What really tipped the balance, I believe, was the thought of turning down such a fabulous opportunity of serving in the greatest ship ever built, a ship that the whole world was waiting to acclaim. After all, you are only young once, and had I turned it down I would never have been able to live with myself.

When my friend came back I told him I was ready to proceed, but that I must go back to Blackheath and resign my job, so that I could not travel up to Glasgow till Monday. This was agreed, and I was whisked off to the doctor. I also met another young fellow who was going through the same process. This was John Rennie, son of a Cunard official, and who was the same age as myself. John and I subsequently became good friends, and when in 1938 my son was born, John stood as his godfather.

When I left the Cunard offices my feet were barely touching the ground. I went into work the following morning in some trepidation, expecting a rocket from Fred Tapper, the factory manager, but he was completely on my side, and seemed genuinely pleased for me. Perhaps he was glad to see me go. I settled up with my landlady and caught a bus for Nottingham.

The reception at home was rather less than enthusiastic, in fact my family were horrified. Horrified. They took the view that I had taken leave of my senses, that I was giving up everything I had worked for—and for which incidentally they had paid—for a mere shadow, a romantic whim. They left me in no doubt that they regarded running away to sea as engine driver stuff, and they doubted very much whether I would ever make the grade as a sailor. It is an understatement to say this was upsetting, for I was very fond of my parents, who had sacrificed much to give me a good education. But there was no turning back now.

When the news got round to my various uncles and aunts my parents' opinion was endorsed. The general feeling was that there was no salt water in the Winter veins, and that within six months I would be running home with my tail between my legs. It was not until many years later that I discovered that my great-great-grandfather, Thomas Winter of Selby, had been a Master Mariner, as had his brother Robert, and that at the end of the 18th century Thomas had been the principal ship-owner in Selby, and quite a character.

The discovery of this fact prompted me to investigate the family history further, and I was amazed and delighted to find that when Drake sailed round the world in 1585 four officers in his fleet were Winters. What is more, one of them, William Winter, became Chief Ordnancer to the Royal Navy, and it was he who altered the whole naval strategy of the day by building smaller and faster ships that would outsail the conventional large troop-carrying men-of-war, and by so doing he helped materially to beat the Spanish Armada in 1588. His theory was that his small fast ships armed with cannon would sink the large and cumbersome ships of the enemy, and the sea would then deal with their men, and this proved to be the case. It was also William Winter who sent the fire ships into Calais among the Spanish Fleet and caused a lot of damage.

When the Armada fight was over Queen Elizabeth met her victorious sailors at Tilbury, and knighted William Winter for the part he had played. Together with his knighthood she gave him an augmentation to his coat of arms, including three Prince of Wales' feathers, and the right, to him and his heirs for ever, to guard the life of the heir to the English throne. So perhaps there was after all some precedent for my action in taking to the sea!

Towering above her Clydebank slip the hull of 'Ship No 534' takes shape but there is still a long way to go (University Archives, University of Glasgow, with approval of the Keeper of the Records of Scotland).

Chapter 2

The ship

When the *Queen Mary* went into service in 1936 the Cunard White Star Company issued a very lush and profusely illustrated booklet commemorating the event, and commissioned H.M. Tomlinson to write an introductory article. The writer visited Clydebank while she was building, and the article he wrote describes his impressions at his first meeting:

'. . . I could hear in the distance that sound so suggestive of diabolic energy, an electric riveter in full career. Then, turning a corner, and giving a shunting engine the room it meant to take in any case, there, mounting over me, apparently based on the cloud of steam from the shunting engine, was the prow of the world's greatest ship.

'The *Queen Mary* was a complete surprise. There could be no argument with that superior and gracious presence. Majesty was there, for her lines were beautiful. Size is but size, but great magnitude is forgotten in nobility of form. You know what it is to turn an unpromising street in Amiens or Seville, and then to see, without expecting it, the soaring lines of the masonry of the medieval cathedral builders. We cannot build these cathedrals today. There are attempts at it, but they are joyless. If the fun these ancient craftsmen found in their faith when lifting those pinnacles can be matched in our age of machines, it is only in the graciousness of the sheer and moulding, and the audacious ascent of her mass, of this latest Atlantic liner. She lifts as buoyantly as the ascent of Chartres. Her weight and bulk are lost in the life of her run and the recession of her tiers of decks, with the three funnels over all. In this immense ship there shows a joy and faith in mechanical power which have transfigured it to beauty. Her very prow, looking down at an observer with the haughty indifference of the

sphinx—the hawse openings are very like eyes, downcast—is superior to questioning.

'We would do well to forget that phrase "a floating hotel". There is no such thing. A ship is a ship. The *Queen Mary* is a personality with her own heritage and attributes. She was born of the science and skill of so many men concerting for a single purpose, and out of tradition and experience reaching so far into the past, that only a skilled examiner may read the signs of her heritage. She is the result of a world of creative influences. She belongs to the ways of peace.

'A ship's response to her creative influences may be of a more subtle refinement. There is an idea, and we dare not question its validity aloud, that the very riveters may give to a ship their own mood. Were they in good spirits when putting her together? It is possible that men contented at their task, inclined to joke and sing while at it, would give a rhythm to their hammering more like praise than that of men sullenly knocking at a grievance. And by the luck of the hammers that built her the *Queen Mary* is an auspicious ship. The men who made her are proud of her, though they would never admit it, being Clydesiders . . .'

The story of how she came to be named the *Queen Mary* is probably apocryphal, but is amusing. Up to this time it was traditional for the names of all Cunard ships to end in 'ia', and for White Star ships to end in 'ic', and the story runs that the Cunard White Star directors wished to

Right *The magnificent sweep of her bridge. The large windows underneath the Bridge are in the Observation Lounge, and those along the ship's side are on the Promenade Deck* (University Archives, University of Liverpool).

perpetuate the tradition by naming her the Queen Victoria. With this in view the chairman approached HM King George V for the necessary permission, but instead of coming out with the actual name they had chosen he said that his company wanted to name their ship after one of the greatest queens that England had ever known. To which the King replied that his wife would be honoured and delighted. And so the *Queen Mary* she became.

As the statistics show, the ship was staggeringly large, and every conceivable superlative was used at the time to describe her. Her gross tonnage of 80,773, which was later increased to 81,237, made her the largest ship in the world, and it was the devout hope of the Cunard White

Star directors that she would prove to be the fastest.

From her earliest days in 1930 her life had been difficult, and in the dark depression of that time she very nearly became a major casualty. At one time, when only partly built, and still simply known as No 534, all work was stopped on her, and for many tragic months her rusting hull lay silently on the stocks at John Brown's Shipyard, while the prophets of doom pronounced that she would never be completed. With the aid of government money however these prophets were proved wrong, and once work on her had restarted the will to succeed was very strong. No wonder therefore that her builders and owners, and indeed the whole nation, were proud of her, and looked to the *Queen Mary*, together with her proposed sister-ship the *Queen Elizabeth*, to establish once and for all the supremacy of British-built ships on the North Atlantic.

After launching and naming by Her Majesty Queen Mary on 30 September 1934 in the presence of King George V and Edward, Prince of Wales, she was never really out of the spotlight, and in fact King Edward VIII paid a long visit to the ship in March 1936 when she was nearing completion in the fitting out basin. As time progressed, so the publicity campaign was stepped up, and by the time she was ready to sail there were very few people in Great Britain unaffected by the excitement.

It is difficult to visualize a ship of such a size, and many publicity pictures were issued comparing her with well-known buildings in London. One such picture showed her alongside St Paul's Cathedral, and another in Trafalgar Square, where she succeeded in dwarfing Nelson's Column. A third one, aimed at the American market, pictured her on end, side by side with the Empire State Building in New York, which she could not quite manage to top.

Even these pictures, fanciful though they were, failed to convey a true impression of her vast size, nor did they even attempt to explain the complexity and scope of her internal architecture. The top deck was known as the Sun Deck, and this was an open promenade on which First Class (or 'Cabin Class' as it was called) passengers could walk round the ship. Above this were the games decks, covering in all a total of two acres, though this figure included parts of

Left *The publicity illustration showing the* Queen Mary *in the unlikely setting of Trafalgar Square* (University Archives, University of Liverpool).

the open deck both forward and aft which came in the Third Class and Tourist sections of the ship respectively. The ship normally carried three classes of passenger, the Third Class being in the forward part of the ship, Cabin Class in the centre section, and Tourist Class aft.

The official booklet issued to all passengers, commenting on the extensive space provided for deck games, claimed that it would take the area of the football field at Wembley Stadium to cover the sports decks and sheltered and open promenade spaces in the three classes. There were in fact three full size deck tennis courts, and one portion of the deck extended the whole width of the ship. Even dogs had their own 80 ft long exercise yard, and a block of 26 kennels.

Approached from the Cabin Class Sun Deck were a number of staterooms, a press reception room, and a photographic dark-room provided for the convenience of passengers; also the radio and Atlantic telephone office in which radio telegrams and telephone calls were accepted while at sea, either from a special telephone call cabinet, or from any stateroom private telephone. In these days of satellite communications this Atlantic telephone call service may seem somewhat modest, but it must be remembered that this was 1936, some fifty years ago, when radio was still referred to as 'the wireless', and was still in its infancy.

At Sun Deck level one also approached the full size squash racquets court which had a gallery for spectators, and the large gymnasium, equipped with the most up-to-date equipment, including horse and camel riding machines, wall bars, vibrating chairs, fencing foils, Indian clubs, a hammer percussion machine, boxing gloves, cycling and hydraulic rowing machines. Bearing in mind the splendid, if somewhat rich, food provided in the ship's restaurants, and the general inactivity of a four-day voyage, many passengers felt it prudent to make use of the facilities available in the gymnasium.

Finally, at the after end of the Sun Deck was the Verandah Grill, affording superb views over the stern of the ship. The company advertised this grill room as being for the service of simple a-la-carte meals for those who did not wish to take their meals in the restaurant. In the centre of the room was a small dance floor in parquetry, and at night time a lively atmosphere was created by ever-changing but discreet lighting. The Verandah Grill was advertised to serve meals from 7.00 pm to 10.00 pm (during which hours there was a cover charge of five shillings) but in practice the room stayed open until the passengers had had enough, usually at about 4.00 am.

The whole superstructure of the ship, culminating in the Sun Deck, rose from the level of A-Deck and was approximately 800 ft long. It was topped by a number of ventilators for the boiler room and engine room fans, etc, and by the three enormous funnels, which were painted in the standard Cunard colours of red with a black top band. Each funnel was large enough to take three double decker buses side by side, though one funnel was partly a dummy, half of it being used as a deckchair store. The Sun Deck, besides being an open promenade, also gave access to the 24 lifeboats, each one of which could accommodate 144 people.

Below the Sun Deck was the enclosed Promenade Deck on which the deck chairs were put out every morning for passengers to take their ease. It was possible to walk right round the Promenade Deck, one circuit being approximately one third of a mile. This deck was glassed in with large windows, the glass being armour-plated and ¾ in thick. Later I will explain why this strength was necessary.

The Promenade Deck contained the principal public rooms. At the forward end of the ship, under the bridge, was the Observation Lounge and Cocktail Bar, a magnificent room having 21 windows, each five feet high, from which one looked right out ahead over the bows of the ship.

Proceeding aft from the Observation Lounge, on the port side were the following: First, the Studio, a specially soundproofed room for private practice by artists during the voyage, and containing a Bechstein boudoir grand piano; a lecture room, equipped with a small cinema screen and two batteries of amplifiers and loudspeakers for lecturers or passengers to show their own films; a writing room, containing a complete range of reference books, ie, directories, year-books, and atlases; and the Library, in which were over 1,400 standard and modern works in English, 250 other works in nine languages, and 400 new and up-to-date works of fiction and general literature.

On the starboard side, matching the rooms listed above, were the Drawing Room, which

Below *A Cabin Class stateroom on B-Deck* (University Archives, University of Liverpool).
Right *Another and differently furnished Cabin Class stateroom* (University Archives, University of Liverpool).
Below right *The Sun Deck* (University Archives, University of Liverpool).

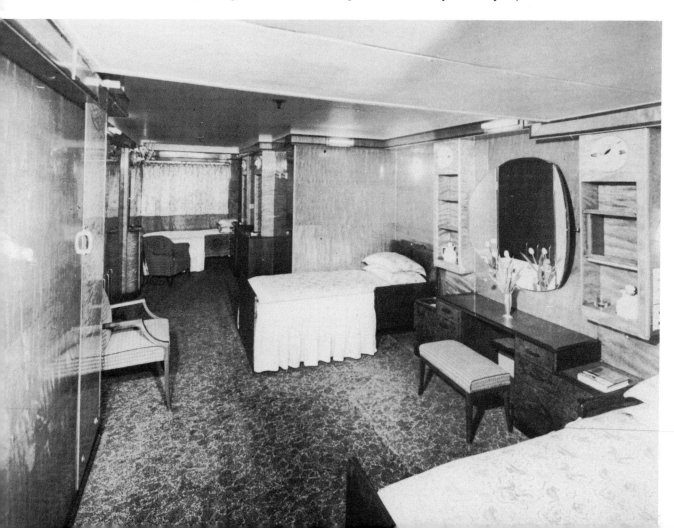

was tastefully decorated and equipped with extremely comfortable furniture, another writing room, and the Children's Playroom. This latter was one of the most fascinating children's rooms ever devised for shipboard, and it contained a large aquarium with tropical fish, a primitive log shack, a long sliding chute, a large doll's house complete with furniture, and a miniature piano. This room was permanently staffed by a trained nurse.

The main entrance hall and shopping centre, which extended across the ship with glass doors leading out each side on to the covered Promenade Deck, and the main staircase leading down,

was a striking and impressive feature. The shopping centre was a veritable arcade of high class shops, prominent amongst these being Austin Reed, the outfitter. Under the heading of 'It may surprise you to know . . .' Austin Reed issued a little publicity booklet written in a pleasantly humorous style, and illustrated by amusing Fougasse drawings. This booklet opened with the following information— 'It may surprise you to know . . .

'That the overall length of the *Queen Mary* is 1,018 feet, or to make it more intelligible, one full and glorious drive of 250 yards, one 50-yard slightly inaccurate approach, one 30 ft chip shot

The ship

Right *The cocktail bar in the Cabin Class Observation Lounge* (University Archives, University of Liverpool).

Left *Port side lifeboats, and a good view of the large boiler room and engine room ventilators* (University Archives, University of Liverpool).

Below *Cabin Class Entrance Hall and Shopping Centre, Promenade Deck* (University Archives, University of Liverpool).

on to the green, and no less than eleven putts of an average of 8 ft apiece!

'That the ship is higher (from keel to funnel top) than St Paul's Cathedral, but quite a different shape.

'That the First Class Restaurant is large enough to accommodate the whole of the first steam Cunarder, the RMS *Britannia*, and also all three of Columbus's ships as well. The latter three vessels, however, being sailing ships, would navigate with difficulty in the pure draughtless air supplied by the air conditioning plant.'

Page 5 of this little booklet tells you that—

'It may surprise you to know . . .

'That there is a squash court on the sun deck, and squash kit to match in the Austin Reed shops.

'That there are special stores aboard for every sort of provision, even down to a cheese store where cheeses are kept at exactly the right temperature.

'That cheeses actually do have an exactly right temperature.

'That the grill room is on the Sun Deck, a fact that sooner or later someone is probably going to try to make a joke about.

'That there is a safe deposit where you can deposit anything you specially treasure, as, for instance, a present for a lady just acquired from the Austin Reed shops.'

The centre pages of the booklet are in the form of a diary covering the four days of the crossing, and are illustrated with four splendid Fougasse drawings showing the gradual transformation of a sober-suited city gentleman into a rollicking Jack Tar. The final advice given is—'It may surprise you to know . . .

'That it's better not to call the ropes *ropes*.

'That it's better not to call the cabins *bedrooms*.

'That it's better not to call them cabins *either*.

'That it's better not to call the decks *floors*.

'That it's better not to call the staircases *staircases*.

'That it's better not to call anything nautical *anything* unless you're certain, and not even then if talking to anyone in a yachting cap.'

The main companion way, or staircase, was flanked by large passenger lifts which connected the Promenade Deck with the Sun Deck above and four decks below, namely Main, A, B, and C decks. Cabin Class passengers had access to all these decks, equivalent to a five-storey hotel ashore. On the after bulkhead, or wall, of the staircase was a beautiful marble plaque of the head of HM Queen Mary, and immediately below this was a glazed frame containing the personal standard of the Queen which she had

Third Class Entrance Hall, C-Deck (University Archives, University of Liverpool).

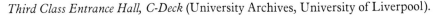

presented to the ship.

Continuing the tour aft from the Main Hall at Promenade Deck level, in the centre of the ship was the Main Lounge, a beautiful and expensively furnished room measuring 100 ft long by 70 ft wide, and in height extending 26 ft up through three decks. One of the carpets in this room was 68 ft long and 26 ft wide, and had a pile one inch thick, and like all the other six miles of carpets it had been specially woven for the ship. This lounge had a fully equipped stage at one end with complete theatre lighting, and was used for concerts and as the Cabin Class cinema.

Aft of the Main Lounge on the port side was the Long Gallery, 118 ft in length, and designed as a convenient room for reading or playing cards. On the other side was the Starboard Gallery, a slightly smaller but no less comfortable reading room and lounge. From these two galleries one could enter the Ballroom, the lighting of which was Thyratron controlled so that when the music was soft and low the lighting followed suit, and when the music was loud the lights were bright.

This was of course before the days of discos and music whose loudness borders on the deafening. In 1936 dance music was relatively quiet and the lighting which accompanied it was equally subdued. Actually the Thyratron control was one of the few pieces of electrical equipment in the ship that did not work very well, and we were continually being called to attend to it. It was, for its day, a fairly advanced piece of electronics, and no one really understood its finer points.

Aft of the Ballroom was the Smoking Room, a big and well-proportioned room, the height of which extended through two decks. It was provided with heavy leather-covered settees and easy chairs, and there was a real coal fire, the intention being to convey the impression of a typical English club or country house. Unfortunately the effect was completely destroyed (for me) by two large surrealist paintings which were as incongruous in this setting as a chromium plated tea trolley in Westminster Abbey.

The next deck down from the Promenade was Main Deck, and this contained the largest and most expensive passenger accommodation in the ship. Special suites were situated on both port and starboard sides, provision being made for two, three, and four roomed suites with private bathrooms and servants' quarters adjacent. All staterooms were of course provided with a private toilet, and most with a private bathroom. Every bed had its bedside telephone, a com-

Front cover of the Austin Reed booklet.

monplace in hotels today, but fifty years ago somewhat of an innovation, particularly in a ship.

Also on Main Deck was situated the Travel Bureau which dispensed information about steamer, rail, and air travel on both sides of the Atlantic, and could also issue tickets and make reservations.

Below Main Deck the decks were lettered— A-Deck, B-Deck, C-Deck, etc. When it is remembered that the lowest deck was H-Deck, ie twelve decks in all, it can be seen that the ship was quite a tall structure. Right through this part of the ship access to the passenger cabins was by means of long wide alleyways, on both port and starboard sides, these being panelled in a variety of most attractive Empire woods.

On A-Deck were more special suites consisting of bedroom, sitting room and private bathroom, and many more luxury staterooms. Also on this deck were the Purser's Bureau; a safe deposit it may surprise you to know . . . . . .

. . . . THAT there are so many things to do in this ship that the following diary may be very much more useful than you think.

1st day	MORNING		MORNING	3rd day
	AFTERNOON		AFTERNOON	
	EVENING		EVENING	
2nd day	MORNING		MORNING	4th day
	AFTERNOON		AFTERNOON	
	EVENING		EVENING	

Above *Centre spread of Austin Reed booklet.*
Left and far right *From the Austin Reed booklet, Neptune and a boy fishing: Fougasse at his best.*

bank consisting of 300 compartments installed for the convenience of passengers possessing valuables or articles of jewellery not required for immediate use; a branch of the Midland Bank for the exchange of money and the transacting of other banking business; a mail and parcels office; and the consulting and waiting rooms of the physician and principal medical officer. Another service for passengers installed on A-Deck was undertaken in the Valeting Service Room, where an expert attendant was available to undertake any type of valeting work.

B-Deck was almost entirely occupied by passenger accommodation, apart from the extensive hairdressing salons and beauty parlour. Some of the prices charged look absolutely ludicrous by today's standards, particularly bearing in mind that the *Queen Mary* was a luxury liner, and that this was the First Class accommodation:

Hairdressing (Gentlemen)
Shaving	1/-
Haircutting	2/-
Shampooing	1/6
Dry shampooing	1/-
Singeing	1/-

Oil shampoo	2/-
Oil shampoo and Vibro	4/-
Scalp massage, hand	2/-
Tonic dressings	6d and 1/-
Mudpack	4/-
High frequency massage	6/-
Lilac and peroxide application	1/6
Hand massage	2/6

Hairdressing (Ladies)

Permanent waving	from 50/-
Finger waving	5/-
Marcel waving	4/-
Waving and curling	5/-
Trimming	2/-
Trim and singe	3/6
Ordinary shampoo	4/-
Tar shampoo	5/-
Henna shampoo	5/-
Camomile shampoo	5/-
Spirit shampoo	4/-
Hand head massage	5/-
Vibro head massage	5/-
Hot oil massage	4/-
High frequency massage	6/6
Bleaching and touching up	from 7/6
Steam scalp treatment	5/-
Brushing and dressing	3/-

Beauty culture

Hand face massage	5/-
Vibro face massage	6/-
High frequency massage	7/6
Eyebrow arching	from 2/6
Mudpack Boncilla and Egyptian	6/-
Magnesia pack	7/6
Peroxide and olive oil massage	4/-
Manicuring	4/-
Hand massage and finger stretching	3/-
Frictions, Coty and Houbigant	3/-
Frictions, Atkinson	1/6
Chiropody	from 5/-

On C-Deck were the Turkish and Curative Baths, the various rooms of which included: frigidarium, tepidarium, massage room and electric bath room, steamroom, calidarium, laconicium, attendant's room. The installation included Turkish bath treatment, complete with cubicles for resting, at the following charges:

Electric bath including alcohol rub	10/-
Turkish bath including alcohol rub	10/-

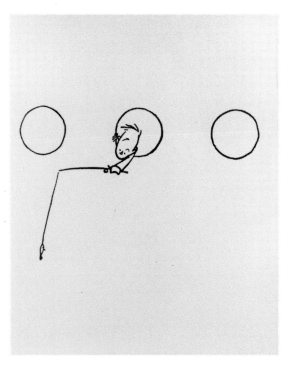

Inclusive charge for Electric or Turkish Bath including alcohol rub for the voyage	25/-
General massage	7/6

A room was also provided for ultra-ray, infra-red ray, diathermy treatment and X-ray, at the following charges:

Local massage	7/6
Ultra Violet irradiation	5/-
Infra-red irradiation	5/-
Ultra Violet and Infra-red	7/6
Diathermy	10/-
X-ray photograph and examination	£1

The above services have been quoted in full, since only by so doing can the extraordinary range of facilities in this ship be appreciated. Fully trained personnel were carried to operate the services, which were all well patronized. An unkind engineer, sweating it out in the heat and noise of the boiler rooms below, claimed that the ship catered for people with more money than sense and commented that down in the boiler rooms much of the heat treatment could be had for nothing.

The Cabin Class swimming pool, which was actually on D-Deck, could be entered through a revolving door on to the balcony on C-Deck, or from the Turkish bath. At the forward end of the balcony was a double staircase leading down to the swimming pool. Cunard were very proud of

Above *Marble plaque of HM Queen Mary, mounted at the head of the Cabin Class main staircase, facing the Shopping Centre.*

Right *The Cabin Class Main Lounge extended up through three decks and was sumptuously furnished* (University Archives, University of Liverpool).

Below *The personal standard of HM Queen Mary presented to the ship and mounted on the staircase below her plaque.*

this pool, the decoration scheme of which incorporated golden quartzite, a stone used in the days of the Pharaohs and never before used in a ship. The pool was certainly impressive, both in decor and in size, but in rough weather it had to be pumped out because quite large tidal waves could be created as the ship pitched and rolled.

C-Deck however was notable for the main restaurant and private dining rooms, the restaurant being the largest room ever built into a ship. It measured 160 ft long by 118 ft wide and was high in proportion. Its decor was superb, as was that of the four private dining rooms, two at each end of the restaurant.

In the restaurant 800 people could sit comfortably at dinner, and when we were running to capacity it was a marvellous sight to see this great room filled with passengers in evening dress, with hundreds of waiters bustling about. English cuisine may lack the finesse and delicacy of the French, but in the *Queen Mary* Cunard catering achieved a very high standard of excellence.

Left *Cabin Class Smoking Room with real coal fire* (University Archives, University of Liverpool).
Below *Cabin Class Gentlemen's Hairdressing Saloon. Most of us had our hair cut here, usually in the afternoons when business was slack* (University Archives, University of Liverpool).

At the forward end of this huge room was a 24 ft by 13 ft painting depicting the North Atlantic, and showing the route of the ship's crossing. On this map was an electrically operated model of the *Queen Mary* in crystal glass which moved automatically across the ocean, and showed passengers exactly where they were. At least this was the theory, but alas the mechanism driving this crystal ship was not all that reliable, and it was frequently necessary to adjust it in the wee small hours when no passengers were about. This adjustment was made from a special trapeze which had to be rigged, and riding this piece of equipment in rough weather was an adventurous pursuit. When the ship was rolling badly maintenance of this model had to be abandoned completely.

The Tourist Class accommodation in the after part of the ship was only slightly less luxurious than the Cabin Class. The Main Deck Tourist Lounge was a large and magnificent room, and the one on A-Deck was equally attractive though

Right *The bronze doors at the after end of the Cabin Class Restaurant on C-Deck. Though massive in construction the artistic detail of their make-up is superb* (University Archives, University of Liverpool).
Below *Forward end of the Cabin Class Swimming Pool* (University Archives, University of Liverpool).

more intimate and somewhat smaller. In addition there was a very comfortably furnished smoking room, a writing room and a library. The Tourist dining saloon was on C-Deck, at the after end of the Cabin and Tourist Class galleys, which were contiguous. There was also a very fine swimming pool. In the *Queen Mary* the standard of the appointments in the Tourist Class was higher than the First Class in many other ships.

Even the Third Class accommodation was of a high standard, The Garden Lounge on Main Deck being a spacious room decorated with plenty of greenery and fresh flowers. On A-Deck there was a large smoking room, and there was another lounge, library, and cinema on B-Deck. Both Tourist and Third Class passengers had their own hairdressing and beauty salons, and of course a Children's Room run by a qualified children's nurse.

A description of the passenger accommodation would not be complete without at least a reference to some of the other ancillary services which were available to passengers. For example there was a small but fully equipped hospital

Left *The Main Restaurant, looking forward, with the map of the Atlantic and the illuminated model of the ship at the far end* (University Archives, University of Liverpool).

Below *The decorative map of the North Atlantic showing the crystal model of the* Queen Mary.

Above *One of the fourteen carved panels by Bainbridge Copnall in the C-Deck Restaurant, illustrating the history of shipping since the Egyptian era* (University Archives, University of Liverpool).
Right *Tourist Class Dining Saloon* (University Archives, University of Liverpool).

containing several beds. This was kept in constant readiness though fortunately it was seldom in use. There was a kosher kitchen, kosher food being available on request. There was a garage, a registered mail room, a strong room, a 700-line telephone exchange, 21 electric lifts, and even a small chapel and altar.

To service all this accommodation, and to look after the 2,000 passengers that could be carried, demanded an extensive organization down below. On D-Deck the Working Alleyway, which was the spinal cord of the ship, ran practically the whole length of the vessel, and off this alleyway it was possible to reach all the offices, store rooms, and workshops for the whole ship, and also the crew accommodation. The three galleys, or kitchens, were on C-Deck, and could serve 3,000 meals at a sitting. They covered an area of one acre, and were completely self sufficient for a ship's complement of nearly 3,500, even having their own bakery which

produced fresh bread and rolls each day. Later on, during the war, when the *Queen Mary* was used as a troopship, the galleys were adapted to serve food for a ship's company of around 16,000.

Fresh food was taken aboard each trip in Southampton, and no one who has ever seen hamper after hamper of live lobsters coming up the conveyor into the ship will ever forget them.

The amount of equipment necessary to service over 3,000 people was also staggering, there being carried 16,000 pieces of cutlery and tableware, 200,000 pieces of earthenware, china and glass, and 500,000 pieces of linen. The ship had her own printing shop, and apart from menus, which were printed daily, we had our

Above *Tourist Class Swimming Pool: the venue for many a midnight dip in New York* (University Archives, University of Liverpool).

Left *Tourist Class Cabin. Officers had cabins similar to these: if anything slightly larger and with bunk curtains* (University Archives, University of Liverpool.)

Above right *Inboard elevation and deck plans.*

Right and overleaf *Each voyage an extract from the Ship's Log was printed and distributed to passengers in the form of a large postcard with a picture of the ship on the back. Three typical examples.*

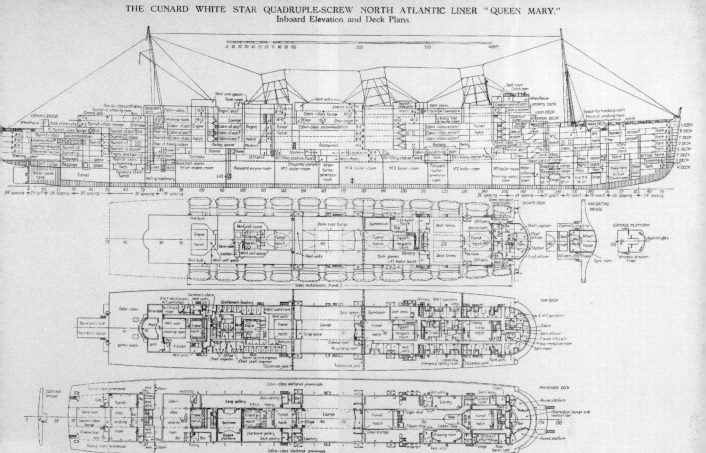

THE CUNARD WHITE STAR QUADRUPLE-SCREW NORTH ATLANTIC LINER "QUEEN MARY."
Inboard Elevation and Deck Plans.

Record Voyage—Cherbourg to New York.

ABSTRACT OF LOG OF THE

Cunard White Star R.M.S. QUEEN MARY

CAPTAIN SIR EDGAR BRITTEN, R.D., R.N.R.

SOUTHAMPTON AND CHERBOURG TO NEW YORK.

1936		Dist.	Latitude N.	Longitude W.	Weather, etc.
Wed.	July 22				At 1.48 p.m. (B.S.T.), Left Berth, Southampton
,,	,,	,,			At 5.43 p.m. (B.S.T.), Arrived Cherbourg
,,	,,	,,			At 8.46 p.m. (B.S.T.), Left Cherbourg
Thursday	,,	23	476	49.55 d.r.	13.50 d.r.	Strong gale, heavy head sea, cloudy and clear
Friday	,,	24	738	48.01	32.20	Moderate breeze and swell, fine and clear
Saturday	,,	25	760	43.28	49.17	Light breeze, slight sea, fine and clear
Sunday	,,	26	734	41.12 d.r.	65.21 d.r.	Moderate breeze and sea, westerly swell, fine
Monday	,,	27	390	To Ambrose Chan. L.V.		

Arrived Ambrose Channel L.V., Monday, July 27, at 12.23 a.m. (E.D.S.T.)
Distance—3,098 nautical miles.   Passage—4 days, 8 hours, 37 minutes.
Average speed—29.61 knots.

ABSTRACT OF LOG OF THE
CUNARD WHITE STAR R.M.S. "QUEEN MARY"
COMMODORE SIR EDGAR T. BRITTEN, R.D., R.N.R.

SOUTHAMPTON AND CHERBOURG TO NEW YORK.

1936	Dist.	Latitude N.	Longitude W.	Weather, etc.
Wed. Sept. 2				At 11.53 a.m. (B.S.T.), Left Berth, Southampton
,, ,, ,,				At 5.32 p.m. (B.S.T.), Arrived Cherbourg
,, ,, ,,				At 8.18 p.m. (B.S.T.), Left Cherbourg
Thursday ,, 3	480	49.56	13.58	Strong breeze, rough sea, moderate swell
Friday ,, 4	714	48.10	31.58	Light breeze, smooth sea, overcast, showery
Saturday ,, 5	727	43.51	48.16	Light airs, smooth sea, confused swell, clear
Sunday ,, 6	731	41.27	64.14	Mod. gale, very rough sea, heavy swell, clear
Monday ,, 7	443	To Ambrose	Chan. L.V.	At 3.00 a.m. (E.D.S.T.) Ambrose Channel L.V. abeam
Total	3,095	nautical miles		

Passage—4 days, 11 hours, 38 minutes.   Average speed—28.75 knots.

ABSTRACT OF LOG OF THE
CUNARD WHITE STAR R.M.S. "QUEEN MARY"
COMMODORE SIR EDGAR T. BRITTEN, R.D., R.N.R.

SOUTHAMPTON AND CHERBOURG TO NEW YORK.

1936	Dist.	Latitude N.	Longitude W.	Weather, etc.
Wed. Sept. 30				At 10.42 a.m. (B.S.T.), Left Berth, Southampton
,, ,, ,,				At 5.08 p.m. (B.S.T.), Arrived Cherbourg
,, ,, ,,				At 7.06 p.m. (G.M.T.), Left Cherbourg
Thurs. Oct. 1	519	49.57	14.59	Fresh gale, rough sea, long S'ly swell, clear
Friday ,, 2	661	48.11	31.35	Fresh gale, rising sea, heavy W'ly swell, cloudy
Saturday ,, 3	647	44.24	46.12	Moderate breeze, sea and swell, cloudy, clear
Sunday ,, 4	742	41.31	62.23	Moderate breeze, slight sea, fine, clear
Monday ,, 5	524	To Ambrose	Chan. L.V.	At 4.58 a.m. (E.S.T.) Ambrose Channel L.V. abeam
Total	3,093	nautical miles		

Passage—4 days, 14 hours, 51 minutes.   Average speed—27.90 knots.

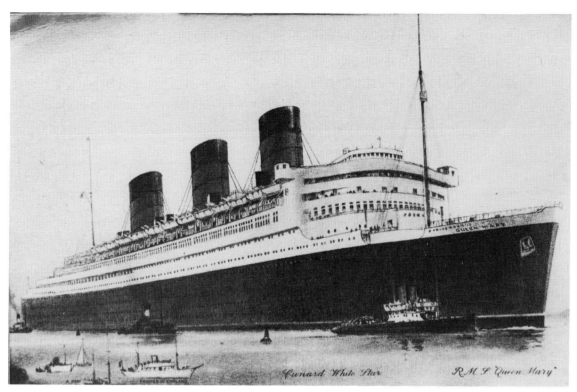

The fine painting of the Queen Mary *on the obverse of the log card.*

own daily newspaper, *The Ocean Times*, a free copy of which was issued to each passenger. At the end of each trip every passenger was given a postcard, bearing on one side a fine picture of the ship, and on the other extracts from the ship's log giving details of the distance run each day of the crossing, the weather, and the speed achieved. These cards were prized as souvenirs of the ship.

To propel this vast complex through the sea smoothly and swiftly required enormous power, and the *Queen Mary* was equipped with four quadruple-expansion steam turbines, each capable of developing 50,000 hp. 'Quadruple-expansion' means that each engine consisted of four separate turbines, the first one taking steam at very high pressure. As the steam was exhausted from this turbine, having lost some of its pressure, it was fed into the first intermediate pressure stage, hence to the second intermediate pressure, and lastly into the fourth and low pressure turbine. Between them these four turbines contained 257,000 blades, each and every one having been tested and fitted by hand. On issuing from the low pressure turbine the steam was exhausted into the condensers, which turned it back into water so that it could be recirculated into the boilers.

Each engine drove its own shaft, these being 2 ft 6 in in diameter, and several hundreds of feet long. Even when developing full power the shafts were only turning at around 200 revolutions per minute, and as the turbines which drove them were rotating at several thousands of revolutions per minute there had to be complicated gearing in between. The largest gear wheel in each gear box was 14 ft in diameter and contained many hundreds of teeth, machined to an accuracy of one thousandth of an inch to ensure perfect meshing with the other gears.

Each shaft terminated in an outsize propeller, made in manganese bronze, and again machined to very fine limits. These propellers weighed about 35 tons each, but were so finely balanced that they could be easily turned. Each one was transported to Scotland from London on a low-loader, causing considerable disruption to traffic on the way, but providing excellent publicity.

The four engines were housed in two engine rooms, and were fed with steam from 24 Yarrow water tube boilers in four boiler rooms, each boiler being capable of supplying 80,000 lb of steam per hour. Three other Scotch boilers in a fifth boiler room supplied steam for the 'hotel services', covering electricity generation, and all

the needs of the passenger accommodation, as distinct from the propulsion of the ship. Oil fuel consumption to produce the total amount of power required was of the order of 1,000 tons per day, at normal service speed.

Electricity was generated in two generating stations, one containing three, and the other four, BTH 1,300 kW turbo-generators. Enough electricity, as the publicity men said, to supply a town the size of Brighton. The two generating stations were quite separate and independent of each other, though they could be linked together if required. One supplied the hotel services and the other powered all the auxiliaries used in propelling the vessel. In port only one station was needed to cope with the load, but at sea both were well loaded.

Left *One of the four propellers, the starboard outer. Each propeller was made from a manganese bronze casting and machined to very fine limits, despite a weight of 35 tons* (University Archives, University of Liverpool).
Below *No 5 Boiler Room, containing six Yarrow water tube boilers, and typical of the four boiler rooms supplying steam for the main propulsion turbines* (University Archives, University of Liverpool).

The *Queen Mary* was actually the first British ship in which all the vital auxiliaries, such as fuel pumps, boiler feed pumps, condenser pumps, etc, were electrically operated, in fact, apart from the main propulsion, which was of course by steam, she was an all-electric ship. The electricity generated was fed into two ring mains which went right round the ship, and there were 52 sub-stations on these mains from which distribution was made. Altogether there were 4,000 miles of electrical cables in the ship, and 30,000 lamps.

The construction and fitting out of the *Queen Mary* provided employment for thousands of workers, not only at Clydebank, but also throughout the country, where no fewer than 200 firms in some sixty cities and towns contributed in one way or another to the ship. I have mentioned above that six miles of carpets of one sort or another were specially woven for the *Queen Mary*, and it could be added that another 13 miles of fabrics for curtains, loose covers, upholstery, and bedspreads were supplied. The internal telephone system, the most complete ever fitted in a ship, accounted for several miles of telephone wire.

The *Queen Mary* was veritably a city that went to sea, a self-contained community catering for

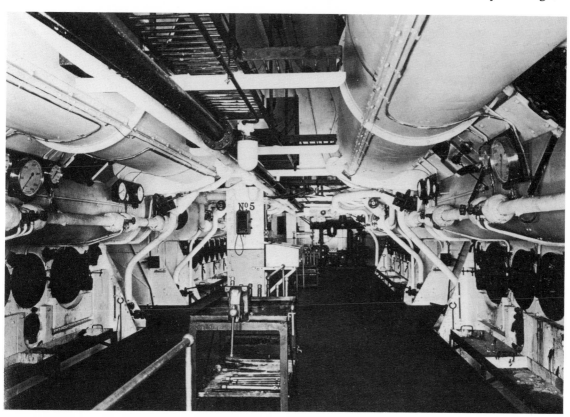

over 3,000 people, many of them in considerable luxury. And yet, for all her size and complexity, she was still a ship, and a very beautiful ship too. Her lines were smooth and satisfying, her hull had a graceful sheer, and many British hearts beat a little faster when they saw her for the first time. She was a great credit to her designers and builders, and was in every sense a 'Royal Ship'.

One of the 52 auxiliary switchboards on the ring main system, distributing power throughout the ship (University Archives, University of Liverpool).

Chapter 3

Decor and art treasures

No British ship ever had as much care and money lavished on its passenger accommodation as did the *Queen Mary*. Cunard claimed that elegance and architectural lightness were essential points in the design of all the 25 public rooms in the ship, and that the decorative themes were modern without being ultra modern. Period styles had been discarded, and the rooms, whilst being perfectly satisfying to the most cosmopolitan conceptions of culture and good taste, were designed to convey an atmosphere of restfulness and comfort. In the commemorative booklet issued by the company (and mentioned already in the last chapter) another article entitled 'A City Goes to Sea' by E.P. Leigh Bennett describes the decor of some of the staterooms:

'But it is towards the staterooms—and what are termed with more restraint merely cabins—that I instinctively turn each time I go aboard. The woodwork throughout these seemingly endless corridors and rooms is, in scope, variety, and beauty, an amazing education in applied joinery work. And behind it all, throughout the ship, has been laid carefully by hand literally miles of soft flannel, so that under no circumstances can there be any creaking, as so often happens when a great ship is at speed. It is perfectly true to say that the forests of the British Empire have been searched for these rare and magnificent veneers. One can think of no more pleasing and at the same time practical form of interior decoration. A vogue will surely be created for this in the homes of Britain and America—set by *Queen Mary* passengers. Over fifty varieties of beautiful woods have been chosen. They measure a million superficial feet, or over 22 acres. If one could place these strips end to end they would reach from Clydebank to St Johns, Newfoundland. Even so, there is not one blemish to be found on all this great surface; discards having been ruthless from the inception of the work.

'To attempt to describe any particular stateroom or cabin is to omit a hundred others, equally attractive. I spent days in a succession of them as they were being built—a craftsman's bench in every one—admiring the meticulous handiwork. For unpretentious luxury and solid comfort there is nothing to equal them afloat. How would you like, for example, to occupy a room at sea such as this?

'Your walls are of ivory-white sycamore, with a faint ripple of grain as the light catches it. (Your neighbour's may be of bird's-eye maple, African cherry, pearwood, Pacific myrtle, or English yew.) All your furniture, of the same, or blending woods, is built in: chests of drawers— as many as in your room at home—of all sizes open silkily, and close with that hand-craftsman's "click". Tall mirrors in triplicate move to your every angle. Deep, long-glass wardrobes light up by themselves as you open their doors; the doors do not swing inwards or outwards if you leave them open, but stay put, in whatever mood the ship may be. Your little built-in clock in the wall ticks soundlessly and is timed from the ship's clock headquarters; there are seven hundred of such set in cabins. Your colour matching telephone stands at your bedside. Your bedlamp is cunningly placed to throw light on the book and nowhere else. Your writing table is cleverly furnished and softly lit. Your bathroom gleams with fastidious gadgets. Your wide bed is of the sink-in-and-stay-there variety. It becomes a divan by day. Your carpet, curtains and chair coverings are of fascinating fabrics, infinitely

varied, cabin by cabin. Nothing obtrudes harshly upon sense or movement. Nothing has been forgotten. Someone gave you flowers when you sailed? A watered niche has been built to take them over your mantlepiece. At night you will hear no sound from the city; your room by day will be gay with light and colour. There is not one dark displeasing patch in any bedroom, nor one discordant note. It is, in fact, a delicately lovely self-contained flat of your own—at sea.'

The souvenir brochure from which the above is taken was well illustrated with colour reproductions of the many paintings and carvings, etc, that had been commissioned from well-known artists, and which were a striking feature of all the public rooms. In all about thirty artists were employed, many of whom were represented in art galleries in the United States as well as the United Kingdom, and were therefore known on both sides of the Atlantic. Their works covered a wide range of styles and catered for a variety of tastes, and many of them excited comments of one sort or another from passengers.

I have already commented on the two surrealist paintings by Edward Wadsworth in the Cabin Class Smoking Room which were not at all to my taste, and which I felt were out of place in their particular setting. Also in this smoking room were some carved and pierced screens in limewood flanking the fireplace, and some electric light sconce fittings. These were modern in conception and beautifully crafted, and in my opinion were much more appropriate to the room.

The large decorative map of the North Atlantic mounted at one end of the Main Restaurant and containing a moving model of the *Queen Mary* has also been mentioned. This was a quite extraordinary work depicting both the New World and the Old, and showing how the *Queen Mary* linked them together. The very size of this map, together with its bold treatment, gave considerable character to the forward end of the restaurant.

As befitted this room, the largest in this or any other ship, there were other impressive works of art. At the far end was a huge mural by Philip Connard entitled 'Merrie England', and at the bottom of this were large double bronze doors by Walter and Donald Gilbert. Round the walls were fourteen carved panels by Bainbridge

Left *'Spring', 'Autumn', and 'Winter': among the most artistic of all the* Queen Mary's *many art treasures were these statuettes by Norman J. Forrest* (University Archives, University of Liverpool).

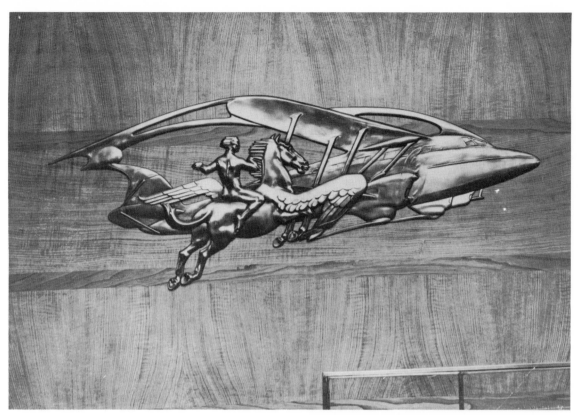

Above *A motif in anodysed aluminium and plaster by
Maurice Lambert, an artist equally at home with many
different materials* (University Archives, University
of Liverpool).

Top left *The special suites were magnificent. This one
had a private dining room as well as a sitting room, and
servants quarters were also provided* (University
Archives, University of Liverpool).

Left *Dining area in one of the special suites* (University
Archives, University of Liverpool).

Right *Decorative bronze statuette by S. Nicholson
Babb* (University Archives, University of Liverpool).

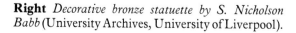

Above *'Madonna of the Atlantic', by Kenneth Shoesmith, a reredos for one of the altars* (University Archives, University of Liverpool).

Left *'Harbour scene' by Kenneth Shoesmith in the Cabin Drawing Room, Promenade Deck* (University Archives, University of Liverpool).

Below *'Evening on the Avon', by Algernon Newton. Long Gallery, Promenade Deck* (University Archives, University of Liverpool).

'Sussex Landscape' by Bertram Nicholls in the Long Gallery, Promenade Deck (irreverently nicknamed 'The Green Cow') (University Archives, University of Liverpool).

Copnall illustrating the history of shipping from the Egyptian era. To my eye these were the most interesting and satisfying of all the works in the ship, but I fear that as they were high up on the walls of this very high room many passengers would fail to appreciate them.

The four private dining rooms each had their own individual paintings which, though the rooms were all the same size, gave each of them a different character. Perhaps the most celebrated, and one that attracted a lot of attention, was a Circus scene by Dame Laura Knight.

In the Promenade Deck Drawing Room there was a very attractive decorative panel over the fireplace. This was a harbour scene with lots of colour, warmth, and flowers, the artist being Kenneth Shoesmith, who also supplied an altarpiece in the Chapel entitled 'Madonna of the Atlantic'.

The Zinkeisen sisters, Doris and Anna, were well represented, Doris having painted fascinating theatrical murals for the forward wall of the Verandah Grill, including the portion of the main-mast that passed through this room.

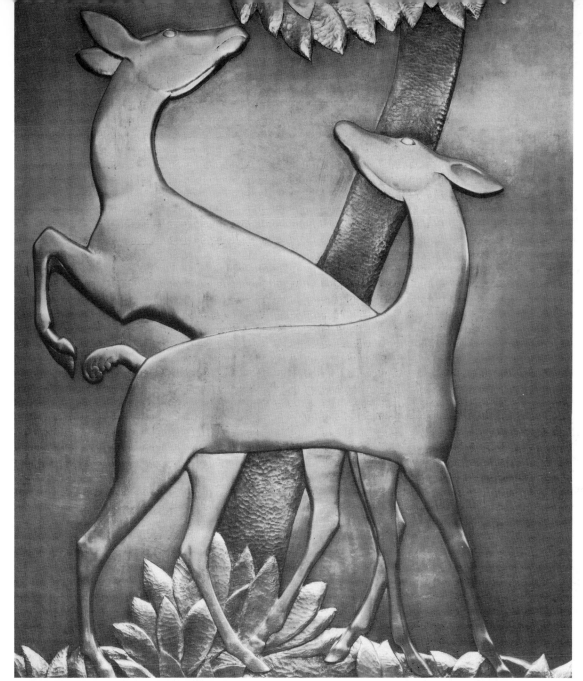

One of the three mural carvings by John Skeaping in the Starboard Gallery (University Archives, University of Liverpool).

Anna's paintings in the Ballroom were equally striking.

The Long Gallery on the port side of the ship contained two large paintings which almost matched each other in their sombre tones. One was called 'Evening on the Avon', by Algernon Newton and this depicted a very peaceful scene on the river just after sunset. The other, a 'Sussex Landscape' by Bertram Nicholls, showed a cow standing under a clump of trees, the Chapel of Lancing College being in the background. The predominating colours in this picture were dark blue and dark green, and it became known (affectionately) as 'the green cow'.

At each end of the Starboard Gallery were two delicately charming flower studies by Cedric Morris, but the most striking works in this room were three large mural carvings by John Skeaping. These were mounted on the inner wall of the room, parallel with the ship's side, and in one tremendous storm when the ship was pitching violently she put her nose down into a mammoth wave which caused such an impact that one of

"THE BABE"

JOHN ROBERTS

MELBOURNE INMAN

WILLIE HOPPE

WALTER LINDRUM

JOE DAVIS

Above *Two of the exquisitely graceful paintings on hide by Margot Gilbert illustrating many different types of dancers. Tourist Main Deck Lounge* (University Archives, University of Liverpool).

Top left *Babe Ruth, one of the most popular baseball players ever: a painting by Tom Webster in the Cabin Gymnasium* (University Archives, University of Liverpool).

Left *Part of the frieze by Tom Webster in the Cabin Gymnasium—this one of billiards and snooker personalities* (University Archives, University of Liverpool).

Above *Brilliantly executed illuminated glass panels by Charles Cameron Baillie in the entrance to the Swimming Pools* (University Archives, University of Liverpool).

Left *RMS* Mauretania *arriving at Rosyth, 4 July 1935, to be broken up: a truly beautiful painting and one very popular with many members of the crew.*

these murals—of three leaping deer—was split from top to bottom. Incidentally, when she hit this wave I myself was on watch in the forward generator room, and the shock was so great that it threw me off my feet.

The Children's Room had murals too, painted scenes of nursery life which amused the grownups as well as the children, and right round the gymnasium was a hilarious frieze painted by Tom Webster, the sporting cartoonist, of boxing, golfing, and tennis celebrities.

The Tourist and Third Class accommodation and public rooms naturally were not so lavishly decorated, but still had their own masterpieces. Among the most delightful were some decorative paintings on hide in the Tourist Main Deck Lounge. These were pictures of dancers, subtle in their colouring and most delicately executed, painted by Margot Gilbert.

One of the most effective pieces of decorative art in the whole ship was also in the Tourist accommodation, at the entrance to the swimming pool. This consisted of a number of illuminated glass panels engraved by Charles Cameron Baillie with various fish and underwater scenes which gave the viewer the impression of looking into an aquarium. These were beautiful indeed.

The Tourist Smoking Room contained an extremely popular picture, a favourite not only with the passengers but also with the crew. This was the painting by Charles Pears of the *Mauretania* arriving at Rosyth on 4 July 1935. A rather sad picture this, for of all the Cunard White Star fleet the old '*Maure*' had inspired more affection than any other ship, and the painting shows her at the end of her career, with the Forth Bridge in the background, arriving at the breaker's yard. She is looking rather bedraggled, with rust trickling down her sides, but is still full of character and dignity. She had held the Blue Riband of the Atlantic for 22 years, and many of the *Queen Mary*'s crew had served in her.

The above short review of the art treasures in the *Queen Mary* is necessarily incomplete and has mentioned only the most outstanding examples. All the passenger accommodation was lavishly but tastefully decorated, no expense having been spared to make this ship the most beautiful and comfortable one afloat.

Chapter 4

Early days

The first few months spent in Clydebank were hectic and bewildering. John Rennie and I were found digs by the company with a foreman electrician at John Brown's Yard, and very comfortable they were too. The house was clean and friendly, and the food was good. For both of us, but perhaps particularly for me, this was an entirely new world, a world of ships and shipyards, and already the excitement and glamour of the *Queen Mary* was beginning to be felt. The completion of this contract, which for so many years had alternately employed and worried the inhabitants of Clydebank, was reaching its emotional climax, and there were very few people in this Clydeside town who were not in some way connected with the ship.

The pace of work on the ship herself was frantic, as she had to be ready to leave in March, and there was still much to be done. At this stage it was reputed that there were 7,000 men working on the ship, and there is no doubt that the majority of them were working very hard. The sailing date had to be met without fail, since she had to go down the Clyde on the top of a spring tide, and there were only two days on which the tide would be high enough. To miss these two tides meant waiting for another six months.

As far as John and I were concerned we were given two weeks to find our way about the ship, and though this may seem a long time it was in fact all very necessary. I have mentioned that there were 52 electrical sub-stations dotted about the ship, and we had not only to find them all—and some of those in the passenger accommodation were pretty well hidden away—but we had to work out the quickest way to reach any one of them from any part of the ship. This involved many weary miles of walking up and down

corridors and companion ways, and the drawing of innumerable diagrams in our note books. But at the end of it we were fairly conversant with the geography of the place, though I must admit that even after two and a half years in the ship there were still some parts of H-Deck, the cargo deck, that I had never visited.

Following the familiarization tour it was necessary to get to know the electrical equipment in the ship, and there was a lot of this. The lighting circuits alone passed through hundreds of fuse boxes, and the position of these had to be known. The air conditioning plant for the passenger accommodation was extensive, and there were many fan rooms tucked away unobtrusively. Add to this the 21 lift houses, cargo and deck winches, boat gear, kitchen equipment, the 700-line telephone exchange, bridge and navigation equipment, together with all the main propulsion auxiliaries, and the many items of spare gear which were stowed away in unlikely places, and it can be imagined that a busy time was had by all. It was for me a strange new world indeed.

Activity aboard reached a new high as the day for us to leave the fitting out basin approached, and it seemed that the whole country was awaiting our debut into the world. The ship had been 'news' for several weeks and as the day drew nearer so the coverage increased, both in the newspapers and on radio. In Clydebank the atmosphere was electric, though feelings were very mixed. Everyone who had been connected with the ship during the last six years and this included a large proportion of the inhabitants of the town—was full of pride and excitement at their achievement, yet there was sadness too. The *Queen Mary* had provided work for the

Above and below *24 March 1936, a momentous day in the life of the world's largest ship. Complete and ready in all respects for sea the* Queen Mary *leaves the fitting out basin in John Brown's Yard where she has dominated the skyline for years. She leaves a big gap in the landscape, and a hole in the hearts of thousands of Clydesiders* (C. W. R. Winter, and University Archives, University of Glasgow).

town, and had been a part of their lives for so long, and indeed a part of the scenery as she had dwarfed everything else in the vicinity of John Brown's Yard, so that there was inevitably a great feeling of regret at her going. Many an eye was suspiciously moist as she finally made her way down the river to the sea.

On board all was bustle and excitement in the knowledge that the long awaited day had at last arrived. All the years of preparation, of hard work, hope and determination, of dismay and despair during the depression when she had to be

Disaster threatens. The channel is barely wide and deep enough to take such a mammoth hull, and bends in the river are tricky. Under the calm control of the pilot, tugs fuss around, working hard to protect her from danger. (University Archives, University of Liverpool).

abandoned, were now culminating in the moment when this mammoth vessel—the like of which had never before been built in a British yard—would leave her birthplace and in an instant would become a live, self-contained and self-sufficient ship; and indeed no ordinary ship, but one on which the eyes of the world were focused, one of which great things were expected.

No doubt those responsible for taking her to sea were also slightly apprehensive about the journey down the river, which to say the least was hazardous. But to a landsman who had never been to sea before this was a most fascinating and exciting adventure, an experience that would surely live in the memory for the rest of one's life.

Gradually the umbilical cords that had tied the ship to the yard for so long were cut one by one, workmen departed by the score, the ship's generators took over the supply of electricity, the catering services began to function, and when the hour finally arrived it was only necessary to drop the moorings and we were free.

Several large tugs had come up from Southampton, and with their help we backed out into the river. The scene was unforgettable. The shipyard and both banks of the river were lined with cheering crowds who had come to wish 'God Speed' to their latest and finest creation, and it was impossible not to have a lump in the throat. Reports later said that a million people had gathered to see her go.

A few miles downstream, on the notorious Dumbarton bend, tragedy very nearly overtook us. For a ship that was over 1,000 ft long the bend is a sharp one, the channel barely wide enough to get her round. There was a hitch on one of the tugs and the strain on a hawser was not taken as quickly as it should have been. The stem of the *Queen Mary* touched the bank of the river and ploughed into the mud. The crowd lining the bank at this point saw the great overhanging bow coming towards them, and they broke and fled in panic across the field. At the same time the tide, which was now ebbing fast, caught the stern of the ship and swung it on to the mud of the other bank. For a few moments, which to those in charge must have seemed like hours, this great ship was fast fore and aft, right across the river, with the water level inexorably dropping. She began to heel over.

Through this crisis the pilot in charge never lost his nerve, never raised his voice. Loud speakers had been rigged in the bow and stern so that he could talk to the tugs, and very calmly he issued his orders. Slowly, but very slowly, the ship was pulled back from the mud until she was afloat again, and after what seemed an eternity our passage down the Clyde was resumed. It was hours later that the full realization of the danger was brought home to us when we were told that

had she stuck there for another twenty minutes the level of the water would have fallen to such an extent that she would not have come off, and at low water she would have broken her back, and become a total loss. What is more she would have completely sealed off the Port of Glasgow until such time as she could have been broken up and taken away.

The most extraordinary feature of this incident which came so near to being a disaster of the first magnitude was that, to my knowledge, it was never taken up by the media and exploited as one might have expected. There was an aeroplane flying overhead at the time taking pictures, and later on we saw some of these which were quite spectacular. We also saw some shots taken from the bows of the ship showing the crowd

The Queen Mary *being manoeuvered by tugs at a turning of the river where she grounded on the soft mudbank shortly after leaving the fitting-out basin. After about half an hour's delay the great ship was back on her course, making her way cautiously round the bend* (Mitchell Library, Glasgow).

lining the bank fleeing away from the river and the approach of this enormous bow.

After this little contretemps the rest of the day was something of an anti-climax. We proceeded serenely down the river and dropped anchor off the Tail-of-the-Bank, near Gourock. The *Queen Mary* was at last at sea.

During the next few weeks we were blessed with fine weather, and this meant that when not on watch it was possible to go up on deck and see what was going on. The Firth of Clyde is an interesting district, and though I had been there before, the present situation was novel. The sea was calm, the scenery magnificent, and the 'working up' of the ship was full of interest. After Blackheath this was Paradise.

At this stage the ship was still being run by John Brown engineers, and had not been handed over to Cunard White Star. Each morning tugs and tenders would fuss round us, bringing last minute stores and visitors aboard, and then we would up anchor and down the Firth for various trials. There had been considerable speculation for some time about the speed that the *Queen Mary* would be able to achieve, so that perhaps most interest centred round the speed trials off

the measured two miles on the Isle of Arran. The media were very interested in this, and one paper even had a light aeroplane buzzing overhead. Those of us on board all had our watches out, and timed her various runs, but opinions varied as to the maximum achieved, some saying it was as high as 38 knots. It all seemed very fast and exciting as we tore up and down, and the wash we created must have caused some very large waves to hit the beach.

The area in which this took place is one of great scenic beauty, and during the trials we saw a good deal of it, the scenery changing with some rapidity as we rushed past the various islands in the Firth of Clyde—Great Cumbrae, Little Cumbrae, Ailsa Craig, and Arran. The weather was ideal for sightseeing with lots of sunshine and a few scattered cumulus clouds, the shadows of which went chasing across the sunlit hills in a most attractive fashion.

The most interesting—and confusing—trial was the last one, which was a 24-hour full speed fuel consumption trial. At a speed of over 30 knots you can go a long way in 24 hours and, as in the engine room we did not know where we were going, the situation was intriguing. We would go

Tearing down the Irish Sea at something over 30 knots.

Above *Southampton East Docks in the 1930s. The Ocean Dock, originally built for the White Star Line, and subsequently the* Queen Mary's *berth, is on the left* (Southampton City Archives).

Below *First appearance in the Solent and local VIPs come aboard* (E. H. Cole).

In the Ocean Dock, Southampton, her berth when in England (E. H. Cole).

on watch in full view of Scotland, and four hours later when we came up for a blow there was Snowdonia. A few hours laters again it would be Land's End. At one point on the eastern horizon could be seen a thin post sticking up out of the water—Blackpool Tower—and later someone pointed out to me a vague blur of mountains on the skyline to port and said they were the mountains of Mourne. Never a dull moment!

When the trials were completed to the satisfaction of everyone we finally said goodbye to Scotland and the Tail-of-the-Bank, and set sail for Southampton, our home port. Here our reception was friendly but restrained. Because of the *Queen Mary*'s draft of 38 ft it was not possible to enter the Solent through the Needles Channel, and consequently we had to come round the Isle of Wight and past the Nab Tower into Spithead. On this route the only tricky bit was immediately off Cowes, where the Brambles Bank had to be negotiated. The channel here is narrow, only 1,000 ft wide, and there is a right-angled turn to be made. To maintain steerage way the ship had to proceed at a minimum speed of 14 knots, so that pilotage on this corner had to be extremely accurate, and in fact the ship had

almost to be spun on her own axis. To stand at an open shipside door looking along the side of the ship and see the Hampshire coastline literally whizzing past as she spun round this corner was quite an experience.

Once round the Brambles it was plain sailing up Southampton Water to the entrance of the Ocean Dock, where a new dockside building had been erected specially for the *Queen Mary*. As we reached the dock six tugs came bustling up and nosed us into the berth. In no time at all we were tied up alongside, the gangways were out, and various VIPs were coming aboard.

For the great majority of the crew this was a happy homecoming, since they lived in Southampton, and in due course most of them were able to leave the ship and go home. But for the Engineering Department there was work to be done, the shore staff came aboard and wanted to see the ship, and it was late before the ship's engineers were able to leave. Even then, one generator had to be kept running to supply the lighting requirements, and of course it fell to my lot, as a junior electrician, to man the switchboard during the night.

The following day sea watches were abolished

and everyone went on to day work, except for the chosen few whose duty it was to keep things running through the night. John Rennie and I, as the only junior electricians with no home ties in Southampton, shared the night shift duty, coming on watch at 5 pm and leaving at 8 am the following morning. This made a long night of it, but there were compensations, not the least being that in the daytime we were able, now and again, to hire a car and explore the New Forest, a district neither of us knew.

One fine and clear night I decided to try to photograph the ship with her floodlights on, and I took my camera round to the far side of the dock and climbed up one of the cranes. Alas I was doomed to disappointment as it was quite impossible to get the whole ship into the picture broadside on without getting very much further away. However the shots I did get were quite impressive and showed up the beautiful proportions of her superstructure.

So time passed pleasantly enough, and the novelty of the situation was still with us. To me, who had been whisked almost overnight from the Black Country, the contrast between the dirt and ugliness of Blackheath, together with the monotony and danger of my job on the test bed at BTH, and the idyllic cruising of the last few weeks in such a fabulous ship, was still bordering on the miraculous.

The routine was broken at one point by a two-day shake-down cruise, on which our passengers were VIPs and members of both houses of Parliament. This was no doubt intended as a goodwill gesture to those who had voted the money spent on completing the ship, but unfortunately the weather was bad and I am afraid that many of our guests did not enjoy themselves overmuch. Some of the stewards did not enjoy themselves either, since the level of tipping was not as high as they felt they could reasonably expect. To this day I do not know where we went on this cruise, but there was a strong sou'-westerly blowing, and the sea was rough. I suspect we did a tour of the Bay of Biscay.

As we rolled down Channel in the teeth of this very fresh breeze we met the German liner *Bremen*, inward bound for Southampton. We passed quite close, and were touched to find that

Title page of the first passenger list ever produced for the Queen Mary, *the inaugural coastal cruise for VIPs.*

INAUGURAL COASTING CRUISE
From
SOUTHAMPTON

THURSDAY, MAY 14th
To
FRIDAY, MAY 15th
1936.

ITINERARY:

				14th May
SOUTHAMPTON	..	..	.. *Depart*	6.00 p.m.
NAB TOWER..	...	..	.. *Passing*	8.30 p.m.
				15th May
LIZARD	..	..	.. ,,	5.15 a.m.
MOUNTS BAY	..	..	.. ,,	6.00 a.m.
LIZARD	..	..	.. ,,	7.00 a.m.
PLYMOUTH	..	..	.. ,,	8.45 a.m.
TOR BAY	..	..	.. ,,	10.50 a.m.
WEYMOUTH	..	..	.. ,,	1.08 p.m.
NAB TOWER..	..	...	.. ,,	3.45 p.m.
SOUTHAMPTON	..	..	.. *Arrive*	6.00 p.m.

TOTAL DISTANCE APPROXIMATELY 470 MILES.

R.M.S. "Queen Mary"

OFFICERS:

Commodore - - -	- SIR EDGAR BRITTEN, R.D., R.N.R.
Staff Captain - -	B. H. DAVIES, O.B.E., R.D., R.N.R.
Chief Officer- -	- C. G. ILLINGWORTH, R.D. R.N.R.
Purser- - -	- C. G. JOHNSON, R.D., R.N.R.
Staff Purser - - - -	- L. E. CARINE
Chief Engineer - - - -	- L. ROBERTS
Staff Engineer - - - -	- W. SUTCLIFFE
Physician and Principal Medical Officer -	- G. A. GOOLDEN
Surgeon - - -	-E. C. BUTLER, F.R.C.S.
Chief Steward - - - -	- A. E. JONES

THURSDAY, MAY 14th
To
FRIDAY, MAY 15th
1936.

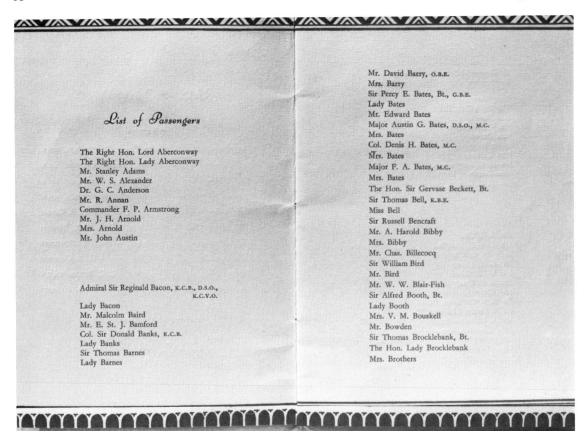

List of Passengers

The Right Hon. Lord Aberconway
The Right Hon. Lady Aberconway
Mr. Stanley Adams
Mr. W. S. Alexander
Dr. G. C. Anderson
Mr. R. Annan
Commander F. P. Armstrong
Mr. J. H. Arnold
Mrs. Arnold
Mr. John Austin

Admiral Sir Reginald Bacon, K.C.B., D.S.O., K.C.V.O.
Lady Bacon
Mr. Malcolm Baird
Mr. E. St. J. Bamford
Col. Sir Donald Banks, K.C.B.
Lady Banks
Sir Thomas Barnes
Lady Barnes

Mr. David Barry, O.B.E.
Mrs. Barry
Sir Percy E. Bates, Bt., G.B.E.
Lady Bates
Mr. Edward Bates
Major Austin G. Bates, D.S.O., M.C.
Mrs. Bates
Col. Denis H. Bates, M.C.
Mrs. Bates
Major F. A. Bates, M.C.
Mrs. Bates
The Hon. Sir Gervase Beckett, Bt.
Sir Thomas Bell, K.B.E.
Miss Bell
Sir Russell Bencraft
Mr. A. Harold Bibby
Mrs. Bibby
Mr. Chas. Billecocq
Sir William Bird
Mr. Bird
Mr. W. W. Blair-Fish
Sir Alfred Booth, Bt.
Lady Booth
Mrs. V. M. Bouskell
Mr. Bowden
Sir Thomas Brocklebank, Bt.
The Hon. Lady Brocklebank
Mrs. Brothers

First page of the coastal cruise passenger list. Sir Percy Bates was chairman of Cunard White Star, Sir Thomas Brocklebank another director.

her band was on deck, playing *God Save the King* as we passed by. She also flew a flag signal consisting of a hoist of about six flags, and this took everyone completely by surprise. I happened to be on the bridge at the time, and marvelled at the chaos that reigned. To begin with, we were end on to her flags, and rapidly separating, since we were both travelling at speed, and it was very difficult to read the signal. Secondly, our flags had never been used before, and some were in the wrong compartments of the flag locker, so that very soon they all had to be brought out, and the bridge was literally ankle deep in flags. By the time a suitable reply had been concocted and flown the *Bremen* was almost out of sight. I forget what the reply was, but believe it to have been a diplomatic version of the message 'And you!'

The interest and respect paid to us by every passing ship, both British and foreign, was really quite heart-warming, and must have owed something to the very efficient and widespread publicity campaign which had been mounted by Cunard.

Gradually, over the next two or three weeks, the ship was worked up to a state of preparedness for the big moment when she would go into regular service, and start earning money. This was the moment that everyone had been waiting for, for many long, weary, and expensive years, the moment when the Royal Mail Steamship *Queen Mary* would be asked to justify the labour and faith that had been poured into her without stint.

The Chief Superintendent Engineer called all the engineer officers together and addressed us in a very soberly phrased speech. He pointed out that the eyes of the world were on this ship and on us, and that the prestige of Britain was at stake. He warned us that the ship would prove to be a hard taskmaster, that with her speed and quick turn round at each end we should find her very

Right *On the trials. From the left—author, John Rennie and George Austin, son of the Chief Superintendent Engineer* (C. W. R. Winter collection).

Electrical engineer officers in 'civvies' before taking over from John Brown's engineers. Standing: second from left, Jock Baxter; sixth from left, Tuckwell; tenth from left, Tyson. On the right, the author; third from right, Sammy Hann. Sitting: on left, Morton; third from left, John Rennie.

tiring to run, and that there would be times when we would be tempted to give in. He emphasized that this must not be allowed to happen, that the sailing schedule had to be maintained regardless of any difficulties which might present themselves. He said that we must be prepared to put the ship before everything else, and that even our homes had to take second place. He invited anyone who was not prepared to accept this challenge to say so now, when he would be found a berth in another ship without any recriminations whatsoever.

There were no takers, but we left the room in a thoughtful frame of mind. Subsequent events proved him to be right in his forecast; she did prove to be a difficult ship to run, and there were times in long spells of bad weather when one seemed to be perpetually tired. I could not help but remember the other somewhat similar occasion when King Henry V left this very port of Southampton to do battle for the honour of England, and in the words of Shakespeare said:
'. . . . and he that hath no stomach for this
   fight,
Let him depart; his passport shall be made,
And crowns for convoy put into his purse;
We would not die in that man's company
That fears his fellowship to die with us.'

Chapter 5

The crew

In their sales literature Cunard White Star always emphasized the importance they attached to the men (and women) who ran their ships. They claimed that Cunarders were the finest ships afloat, but that the ships were only as good as the men who ran them.

'. . . much more than steel goes into the making of a transatlantic liner. Nor is it only the men of the decks or the bridge that feel the influence of a tradition that is older than they. Stewards and stewardesses share the same heritage. . . Many of them have had fathers and even grandfathers in the Line. "Service" and "Seamanship" after all are but two different phases of the same ideal . . . It is this, the British tradition, which distinguishes a Cunard White Star crossing. Its influence cannot be escaped from quarterdeck to galley. Even though ships are built as gigantic and wondrous as the new superliner *Queen Mary*. . . it's still the men that count.

'Every navigating officer in the Cunard White Star fleet, from the Junior Third upwards, holds a master's certificate and is officially qualified to take command. All of the twenty-four Captains are officers in the Royal Naval Reserve. Twenty-two have the Royal Decoration. Six are Officers of the Order of the British Empire. Two have the Distinguished Service Cross. One is a Baronet. One is Aide de Camp to His Majesty King Edward VIII . . . an honour, the highest that can be conferred, granted to one only in the merchant service.

'And yet this imposing list tells but part of the story. Titles can be bestowed in a day, new and resplendent as the ships these men command. Older far, and beyond the power of any man to give, is the heritage of the sea . . . the breeding, the instinct and the training that make a true seaman.

'May you, sometime, find yourself comfortably ensconced in the smoking room of a giant Cunard White Star liner . . . and give a thought to what goes on on the bridge. There, in spite of all the marvellous modern improvements, the discipline and unrelenting vigilance of the old-time merchant marine still rule. The ship, perhaps, is feeling her way in thick fog . . . but you know that the Commander watches with a seaman's eyes and ears. You come to shallow waters . . . and though the fathometer tells him his soundings almost to an inch, he will have the quartermaster heave the lead from the "chains" to confirm his depth by the line and to check his bearings by samples of the ocean floor. His course is automatically controlled by the Sperry Gyroscope. The radio direction finder gives him his ship's position with uncanny speed and accuracy. Submarine signals warn him instantly of any approaching vessel. Yet he and his First Officer and the two look-outs in the crow's nest are intent on every shape and sound . . . theirs is the final responsibility.

'No one, after all, will ever find a substitute for fidelity and vigilance. The marvels of science may aid immeasurably, but it is still men who navigate a ship. And many an able commentator has conferred upon Cunard White Star officers the most eloquent of all epithets . . . "Salt of the Sea".'

So ran the publicity blurb about the glamour boys of the transatlantic liner, the deck officers. But they were, of course, only a part of the total complement of officers, and numerically a small part at that. In the *Queen Mary* there were altogether about 110 officers, of whom only a dozen

Above *The engineer officers of the* Queen Mary *in 1936, a group photograph taken in New York. Roberts and Sutcliffe, Chief Engineer and Staff Chief respectively, sitting in the centre. John Rennie is in the first standing row, fourth from the left. The author stands in the back row, fifth from the left.*

Right *Author on the wing of the Bridge having just repaired a faulty signal light.*

were deck officers. Of this huge total 84 were engineers, but we were seldom seen by the passengers, spending all our working life down in the bowels of the ship. Other officers included pursers, doctors, and the chief steward, and though we all wore basically the same uniform we could be distinguished, not only as to our function but also as to our rank, by the bands of gold lace on the lower part of our sleeves, and the different colour of the narrow strip of velvet in between the gold lace bands. The little booklet issued to passengers printed the following guide to identifying officers:

Commodore—One broad gold lace band.
Staff Captain—Four rows gold lace, straight.
Chief Officer—Three rows gold lace, straight.
Chief Engineer—Four rows gold lace, straight, with purple velvet between.
Staff Chief Engineer—Four rows gold lace, straight, with purple velvet between.
First Senior Second Engineer—Three rows gold lace, straight, with purple velvet between.
Purser—Three rows gold lace, straight, with white velvet between.
Physician and Principal Medical Officer—Three rows gold lace, straight, with red velvet between.

Surgeon—Three rows gold lace, straight, with red velvet between.
Chief Steward—Three rows gold lace, zig-zag.
Company's Representative on Board—Three rows gold lace, straight, with blue velvet between.

When officers are in White uniform, similar badges of rank will be shown on the shoulder straps instead of on the sleeve of the coat.

The rank of Commodore was peculiar to the *Queen Mary*, the Captain of which was also Commodore of the Cunard White Star fleet, our first Captain being Sir Edgar Britten. As was to be expected, such a lordly creature was not very often seen by junior officers in the engine room, but those who had sailed with him in other ships spoke well of him, and he certainly seemed to present the right image to the world.

The responsibility he carried was fearsome—seven and a half million pound's worth of ship, and the lives of up to 3,500 human beings, in all weathers—and he had to keep to a time schedule as rigorous as that of a No 11 bus. Sadly it ultimately proved too great a burden for him, and one morning just before we sailed from Southampton his steward took him his cup of tea and

found him dead in his bunk.

In the Engineering Department we had a Chief Engineer and a Staff Chief Engineer, the latter's duties being presumably to look after the staff, though I must confess that the division of responsibility between the two always remained something of a mystery to me. They each had a suite of rooms, and both seemed to do a fair amount of entertaining of important passengers. Obviously the ultimate responsibility for keeping the engines running lay with the Chief, who was a Welshman, but the Staff Chief, who was a Yorkshireman, frequently poked his nose into things in the engine room, and words were occasionally exchanged.

Looking back after all these years I am bound to say that they were a strangely ill-assorted pair, both Roberts (the Chief) and Sutcliffe (the Staff) exhibiting their own national characteristics. They were both rather short in stature, and Sutcliffe at least used to strut about a bit. They both had much scrambled egg on their caps, and both wore huge gauntlet gloves on the rare occasions they visited the engine rooms. Once, when in the Chief's private sitting room mending a faulty electrical fitting, I tried on his cap which was lying about. It did not suit me.

The Chief Electrical Engineer, Sammy Hann, who was my immediate boss, was a different sort of character, being slim, dark, and dapper, with well plastered down hair. He was what is known as a snappy dresser, and we seldom met him in the dirtier parts of the ship. In an unguarded moment I heard him confess that he avoided going into the boiler rooms since the slightly higher atmospheric pressure there hurt his ears. He was not a man for whom everybody had a tremendous regard, but he must have impressed his superiors to have been appointed to this, the plum electrical job in the fleet.

Hann was a Cunard man, whereas his second in command, Tyson, came from a White Star ship. Tyson was a big, but gentle, man, universally liked, and I suspect he sometimes had to act as a buffer between Hann and some of the senior engineers. Many of the electricians, particularly those with a White Star background, were of the opinion that Tyson should have been Chief.

There was always a slight feeling of bitterness amongst the ex-White Star engineers concerning the amalgamation with Cunard. They felt that the White Star Line had not been treated with complete fairness, and that the pride of the White Star fleet, the *Majestic*, had been scrapped prematurely. In fact, the rather wry joke was that there had only been one thing wrong with the *Majestic*, and that was the colour of her funnels.

Under the supervision of the Chief and Second Electricians, who worked daytime hours, came the watch-keepers, headed by three Third Electricians, Walter Kay, Harry Baker, and Alf Timewell, and so on down the line, there being three Fourth Electricians, three Fifths, and so on, until the lowest form of electrical life was reached, namely John Rennie and myself.

We were a very varied bunch—all sorts and

conditions of men in fact—many of whom have remained in my memory. For example, there was Mr Tuckwell, one of the 'Fourths', who was responsible for supervising the work of the juniors on switchboard duty in the generating stations. Tuckwell was a gentle soul, of a religious turn of mind, and straight as a die. You did not swear when talking to him, and I often wondered what on earth had caused him to be a sailor. On one occasion when he visited my switchboard I used in conversation a fairly common expression, but modified it slightly to suit his delicate ears, and likened someone to a 'blue-nosed fly.' He heard me out and then solemnly corrected me, saying 'I think the expression is a "blue-*arsed* fly".' And then he started to chuckle, not at my story, but at his own daring, until finally, being unable to keep a straight face, he had to leave me.

At the other end of the scale was a man whose nickname was 'Tubby', who was coarse and vulgar to the point of being revolting. He was frequently drunk and was continually boasting of his prowess with women, his prime boast being that he was unfaithful to his wife within 24 hours of marrying her.

In between were a number of very good fellows with whom it was a pleasure to work. They included Jock Baxter, who had a great sense of humour and was always cheerful; Morton, who paid me a compliment by apologizing for having thought when he first met me that I would not make the grade as a sailor; Hogan, the Irishman, who taught me the salutation 'Hallo there!', and whose special care in the ship was the spare gear which was stowed away in the most unlikely places; Johnson, who, when I asked innocently in the Mess Room one day 'How's the ox-tail?' immediately said 'It's on the bum!'; and many, many others.

Amongst them I must not forget my room-mate Jackie Brinton, whose ruling passion was betting on horse racing. At the beginning of the racing season he would pick a handful of likely horses and meticulously monitor their careers, noting each detail of their every outing, the weight they were carrying, the jockey, the going, etc, etc. He never let a day go by without placing at least one bet, very often wagering far more than he could afford, and his life as a result was mercurial, being a quick succession of peaks of delight and depths of despair.

At this time the wages paid in the British Merchant Service were pretty poor, and though the Cunard company was considered one of the better payers, and the *Queen Mary* was the highest paid ship in their fleet, the money was still far from good. John Rennie and I started on £9 per month, plus keep—not £9 per *week*, mark you, but per month—less stoppages, of course. The next grade up earned £11 per month, and so on up the scale, each grade earning a few pounds more than the one below. The Chief Electrician was getting all of £400 per annum, and the Chief Engineer £1,250.

Everyone knew what everyone else was getting and the system was quite rigid. There was no question of asking for a rise, you were paid at a certain level and that was that. The only saving grace was that if a man above you went on leave you automatically went up a grade and while he was away earned a higher wage. Obviously when you were the lowest of the low and on the lowest rung you always profited, no matter who went on leave. Actually, it was not quite as bad as it sounds, for when I got married after being at sea for about a year I was earning £14 per month, and once for a short period reached the dizzy heights of £19.

The total number of crew carried varied according to the number of passengers, and since during the first year or so of her life at least the *Queen Mary* was fully booked, so the crew was at a maximum too. By far the greatest number were engaged in looking after the passengers, and these—mainly stewards, stewardesses, waiters, cooks, and chefs—numbered over 1,000.

Of all the crew the stewards were the most affluent, but not because their wages were high. Their basic wage was £4 per month, but they had access to a large reservoir of wealth—the passengers—and tipping in the *Queen Mary* was of a high order. A 'tronc' system ran throughout the catering department, so that those not in contact with the passengers could still get a share, and the man who actually received the tip had to give much of it up to the colleagues who were behind him. In this way everyone, from the lowest kitchen hand up to the Chief Steward himself, participated, and it is a fact that after 18 months service in this ship this latter dignitary was able to take early retirement.

Nevertheless the stewards themselves were affluent. Whether the largesse they received was on such an unprecedented scale that they were able to put a little extra on one side for themselves I cannot say, but they were certainly affluent. One I knew, who serviced a few cabins on Main Deck, told me a sad story one day. Apparently he had two sons, the elder of whom was up at Oxford, and had just had an accident in his car, which was an MG, one of the most sporty cars of

The engineer officers' Mess Room. There were 84 of us altogether, though for obvious reasons we never all dined at the same time (University Archives, University of Liverpool).

the day. This young gentleman was wanting to borrow his father's car, which was a large family Austin, until such time as his MG was repaired, and though his father was resisting he was expecting to have to give in in the end. While he was telling me this he was making the beds and emptying the ashtrays, and other things, and it must be remembered that this was 1936 when not every family had a car, and when two-car families were few and far between. His younger son was a bit of a rip too, but was not in trouble at the moment. He was still at school—at Oundle.

When we arrived back in Southampton each trip there was always a line of cars on the dockside. These were the stewards' wives, waiting for their lords and masters. Sir Edgar Britten, Captain of the ship and Commodore of the Cunard White Star fleet, used to come down the gangway with a parcel of dirty washing under his arm, and get on a tram.

Chapter 6

The North Atlantic

The Atlantic Ocean, so we are told, covers an area of 30,000,000 square miles, but this is such an astronomical figure that it is difficult to comprehend. To cross the northern part of the ocean, from the Bishop Rock in the Scilly Isles to the Ambrose Light, just off Long Island and the entrance to New York Harbour, involves a journey of about 3,100 miles, and even this figure is not easy to digest. To make an easier comparison, imagine travelling in a car at a steady speed of 35 miles per hour (which is about the speed maintained by the *Queen Mary* in good weather) then if you travelled from London up to Edinburgh, then back to London, up to Edinburgh again and back to London once more, you would have covered a distance equal to about halfway across the Atlantic. At this mid point in the ocean the nearest land would be over 1,000 miles away in any direction—except of course vertically downwards where it was only about four miles away!

As can be imagined, in such a remote expanse the weather can at times be extremely fierce. The prevailing winds are westerlies, and when they blow there is nothing, but absolutely nothing, to break their force. The North Atlantic is notorious for its wild weather, and its sudden changes from calm to storm, and the waves that can be generated on the surface of the water literally have to be seen to be believed. Text books will say that the maximum size of waves will be about 50 ft high and 600 ft long from crest to crest, but in the chapter on bad weather I will tell you about waves bigger than this.

The North Atlantic also has several tidal currents, two of these being particularly significant to ocean voyagers, the most remarkable and best known being the Gulf Stream. This has its origin in the Gulf of Mexico, hence its name, where warm water entering from the Caribbean Sea is raised to a high temperature and creates two currents which between them set about three quarters of the waters of the Gulf of Mexico in motion. These two currents ultimately unite about 60 miles west of Havana, and give rise to the Gulf Stream.

The Stream passes along the shores of Cuba; through the Straits of Florida; along the shores of Georgia and Carolina; bends round gradually to the north-east, almost touching the bank of Newfoundland; and after changing direction to the east and south-east, crosses the ocean and passes near the Azores. The current is about 100 miles in breadth and at its commencement its velocity is small, but in some parts it reaches a speed of 5 miles per hour. The water in the Gulf Stream is of course warmer, the temperature being anything from 8 to 12 degrees Fahrenheit higher than in the surrounding ocean, but apart from the warmth it is always possible to tell when you are in the Gulf Stream by the amount of seaweed being carried along.

It has long been supposed that the warm waters of the Stream are responsible for the mildness of the climate in parts of the British Isles and northern Europe, but there are other theories claiming that this is due more to the flow of equatorial water towards the pole. Whatever the truth of this the Gulf Stream is certainly responsible for some of the sudden and violent weather changes which occur in mid-Atlantic.

The other current which is of significance to North Atlantic travellers is the Arctic Current, which brings icebergs down in a south-westerly direction from the Arctic Ocean all the way to Newfoundland. In the short summer season these bergs, together with those emerging from the St Lawrence River, constitute a very real menace to shipping in these waters.

Icebergs can be of such a colossal size—well over a mile in length and several hundred feet high—with up to nine times as much bulk in the water as is visible, that even the largest and stoutest ships stand no chance in a head-on collision, as the *Titanic* found to her cost. As the icebergs drift south so they reach warmer waters and gradually melt, and the route taken by the great liners from Europe to New York tended to skirt the danger area. In summer, when ice could possibly be about, the route was always changed to be further to the south. The presence of ice could usually be foretold by the fog which very often surrounded the larger bergs, and the general clamminess of the atmosphere.

Men have been crossing the North Atlantic for centuries, and though Christopher Columbus is credited with being the first European to discover the New World, on the occasion when in October 1492 he first reached the West Indies, it is now believed that the Vikings may have penetrated to Canada via Iceland and Greenland many centuries before. However, it was the discoveries of Christopher Columbus and other explorers of the 15th and 16th centuries that opened up the New World to European adventurers. By the beginning of the 17th century colonization of the North American continent was in full swing.

The ships of those days were, to our minds, exceedingly small, frail, and unseaworthy for tackling such a formidable crossing, and indeed many that set out were destined never to arrive at their destination. Size is of course not everything, and the North Atlantic has within recent years been crossed in many very small vessels, including rowing boats, but the ships which first established a passenger service to America from Europe were often of only 300 to 400 tons and were square rigged, which made them very inefficient when dealing with the prevailing head winds of the west bound crossing.

As traffic became heavier, and competition stronger, so ships began to increase in size, efficiency, and the amenities that they could offer. Passengers were well aware that the Atlantic was a stormy ocean, but they came to demand comfort, safety, speed, and a reliable service that would run to a schedule all the year round, regardless of the weather. The Cunard company and the White Star company, long before their amalgamation into Cunard White Star, had both pioneered the North Atlantic

route, and their success was one of the reasons for the rising competition from other nations.

In the race for supremacy, during the 19th century, development became very fast. It was not until 1838, less than 100 years before the *Queen Mary* sailed, that the first ships crossed the Atlantic under steam power. These were, of course, wooden paddle steamers. In 1840 Samuel Cunard inaugurated his first regular transatlantic service with four ships, each of 1,100 tons, building on the pioneering work of the diminutive *Sirius* and Brunel's innovative *Great Western*. At this time it was still believed that to build a ship of iron was impossible—it was only common sense that wood floated but iron would sink—and the first iron Cunarder, the *Persia*, did not come until 1855. Cunard was also experimenting with a new-fangled device, the screw propeller, which many experts said would never work, but which ultimately supplanted the paddle wheel entirely. From this time on development was particularly rapid.

The *Servic*, of 7,000 tons, and capable of 16 knots, went into service in 1881. The *Umbria* in 1884 had a speed of 21 knots, and reduced the Atlantic crossing to six days. She and her sister-ship the *Etruria* ran a scheduled service which was remarkably reliable for that day and age.

In 1899 the largest ocean liner was the White Star *Oceanic* of 17,000 tons, but eight years later the size had jumped to 32,000 in the *Mauretania*. She was followed in 1911 by the *Olympic*, 45,000 tons, in 1912 by the *Titanic*, 46,000 tons, in 1913 the German *Imperator* (later the *Berengaria*) 52,000 tons, in 1922 the *Bismarck* (later the *Majestic*) 56,000 tons, and in 1935 by the *Normandie*, 79,000 tons. From wooden sailing ships to 79,000 ton steel steamships in under 100 years is a fantastic rate of development.

It was at this point that the *Queen Mary* made her entry, her ultimate objective being to provide, together with another ship of the same size, a reliable and fast transatlantic service which would replace the ageing *Mauretania, Aquitania,* and *Berengaria,* and re-establish British supremacy on the North Atlantic. A more immediate target, and one that had good publicity value, was to capture the 'Blue Riband of the Atlantic' for the fastest crossing, a record held by the French *Normandie*. Though the second ship in this plan, the *Queen Elizabeth*, was ultimately built, she was overtaken by world events in the shape of the war of 1939-45, by the end of which long range aircraft had been developed to the point where it was possible to cross the Atlantic quickly and safely by air, and this spelt the end of the monopoly enjoyed by the Atlantic liner. Hence, the *Queen Mary* represented the climax of the development of super liners. There is no doubt that in her time she was the greatest ship ever built, but she marked the beginning of the end of an era, and we shall never see her like again.

But even in the *Queen Mary*, the largest and most powerful liner to that date, there were many times in mid-Atlantic when one was very conscious of her insigificance in comparison with the stupendous forces of nature with which she had to battle, times when it seemed a miracle that she could stay alive amid the noise and fury of the elements, when sea and sky were merged into one bewildering composite, half air, half water, and the sheer noise of the storm battered at the senses.

At such times it was impossible to recall the peace of the many calm days when the deep midnight blue of the sea was in startling contrast to the cerulean sky and the intense white of the bow wave, or in the warm, almost sub-tropical, moonlit nights when the wake was full of phosphorescence. These extremes of weather, and every shade of mood in between, were typical of the North Atlantic, which though often lacking in charm, never failed to fascinate.

Chapter 7

The maiden voyage

The passenger list on the maiden voyage from Southampton to New York read like so many pages from *Who's Who*. It was, to be quite honest, an extremely snobbish occasion. The publicity campaign had been so telling that public interest in the *Queen Mary* had been whipped up to fever pitch, and to very many people the most desirable thing in the world was to travel in her on the maiden voyage. There had been a stampede for reservations, and anyone who thought he was someone had applied for tickets. Every berth in the ship was taken and there were many disappointed would-be passengers.

The morning of 27 May 1936 dawned bright and fair, the weather forecast was good, and the omens for a successful voyage were propitious. Some passengers had joined the ship the night before, but the boat trains from Waterloo brought the great bulk of them, smart looking trains which puffed slowly into the docks, and set down their excited human cargo only a few yards from the ship. Stewards in smart new uniforms bustled about on the dock side, and a never ending stream of impressive looking suitcases and cabin trunks trundled up the conveyors into the ship. Inside the ship all was excitement; everyone seemed to be moving at the double, friends saying goodbye to friends and trying to see as much of the ship as possible before having to go ashore, gasps of astonishment arising on every side. At times it seemed impossible that the atmosphere would ever return to normal.

The only places where calm prevailed were the engine rooms, boiler rooms and generating stations. Here there was no excitement, no streamers, no noise. The 8 to 12 watch went about their routine jobs quickly and efficiently.

In the boiler rooms the engineers watched pressure and temperature gauges as the head of steam was gradually raised, in the generating rooms the electrical load was rising too, and the engineers were running up another turbine against the time when the ship began to move and additional electrical load came on them from the engine rooms. On the engine room starting platform the telegraph from the bridge stood at 'Stand-by', and the watchkeepers continuously monitored instruments which told them what was happening in boiler rooms and generating stations, ready at a moment's notice to carry out instructions passed to them from the bridge.

In due course, in mid-morning, the call came over the ship's loudspeakers 'All ashore who are going ashore', and in a last frenzy of excitement friends bade farewell to friends and were shepherded down the gangways to the mundane environment of the dock side. One by one the conveyors and the gangways were withdrawn from the ship's side until only one gangway connected her with England. Shipside doors were shut and fastened, and finally the sole remaining gangway was swung away and the door closed. The *Queen Mary* was in every respect ready for sea. Our tugs came fussing into the dock and took up their positions, moorings were singled up and then cast off, and down in the engine room the telegraph sprang into life with a clanging of bells, the pointer coming to rest on 'Slow Speed Astern'. Slowly the great ship began to move, the tugs gently but firmly coercing and guiding her out into Southampton Water where they turned her so that she was facing the sea, and her future. With one long blast from her deep-throated whistle we said goodbye to Southampton and the thousands of cheering people who

Above *The start of the maiden voyage as seen from The Parade, Cowes. One man thought it was all a lot of unnecessary fuss!* (University Archives, University of Liverpool).

Above right *Cover mailed from the ship on the maiden voyage.*

Right Queen Mary *letterheads.*

had crammed every vantage point to see us leave.

Among the passengers we carried on this trip were a film crew who were intent on capturing every magic and memorable moment of the voyage, and subsequently a film called '*Wonder Ship*' was released and shown in cinemas up and down the country. In this film I made an unwitting appearance—pointing out the Statue of Liberty in New York harbour to two passengers, a sight I was also seeing for the first time.

We also carried Mr Henry Hall's Dance Band, one of the leading orchestras of its kind at the time, as it was planned to relay dance music by wireless each night. This was something of an innovation, daring at the time, and it is difficult now, with satellites orbiting overhead and television pictures flashing round the world, to realize that in 1936 radio communication between the two continents was not yet commonplace.

Another thing carried by all the passengers and many of the crew in their hearts was a firm con-

viction that on this trip we should shatter the existing transatlantic record and triumphantly snatch from the French liner *Normandie* the coveted Blue Riband. But the Cunard directors were wiser than we. The *Queen Mary* was getting all the publicity possible as it was—why pile Pelion on Ossa by adding a record run? It would be better to wait until the ship was slipping from the headlines, and at this point break the record and so bring her back into the public eye. And so it turned out that it was another two months before in fact we became officially the fastest ship on the North Atlantic.

It was somewhat surprising to find that the Cunard Head Office in Liverpool exercised a very tight control on the movements and performance of the *Queen Mary*. Each trip they laid down the course that was to be followed, this being a 'dog-leg' with a distinct turning point about two-thirds of the way across, and varying in longitude with the seasons of the year and the breaking up of the ice in the St Lawrence River.

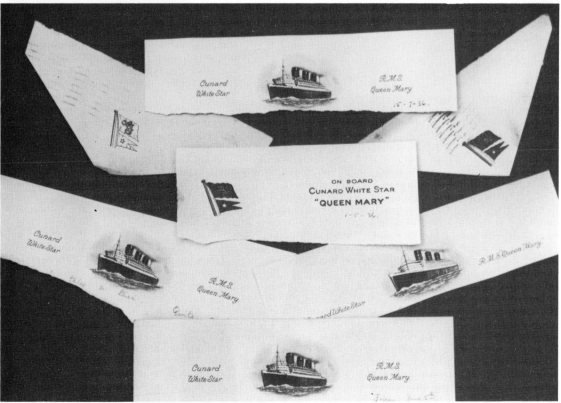

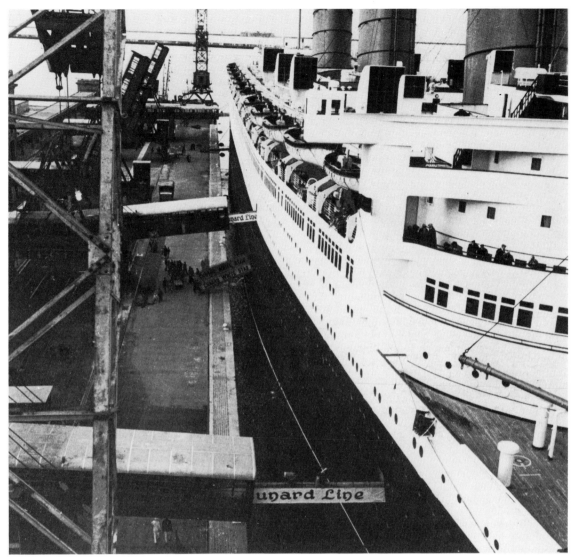

Cherbourg. The three gangways, all too short (University Archives, University of Liverpool).

Every spring this ice is spewed out into the Atlantic, and the big bergs drift southwards across the shipping lanes.

There was however little thought of fog and ice in the *Queen Mary* on this sunny 27 May. During the afternoon we arrived in Cherbourg to another reception, with many boats in the harbour to greet us. The French had also constructed a special dock building containing all necessary port facilities, and quite a few passengers were to join the ship here. This dockside building contained a rather splendid gangway, very wide and sumptuously appointed, which slid out silently from the side of the building and was designed to fit exactly into our shipside door. Unfortunately, there had been a miscalculation somewhere, and although it was in perfect alignment it was about six feet short, and a very makeshift arrangement had to be hurriedly rigged to span the gap.

Our stay in Cherbourg was only for a few hours, and in the early evening we were off again, heading west out into the Atlantic, on the major part of the crossing. Down in the engine room, as we cleared the harbour entrance, the telegraph rang 'Half Speed Ahead', and a little later 'Full Speed Ahead.' A few more minutes and the signal 'Full Away' was received, this indicating that we were now clear of danger, the stand-by watch could stand down, and that all being well the steam valves would not have to be touched again for another four days. That evening there

Above *Part of the maiden voyage reception in New York: some of the Wilson Line's Hudson River day boats, normally employed on day trips up river to Niagara (University Archives, University of Liverpool).*
Right *At anchor off Staten Island, New York Bay, awaiting Customs, Health and Immigration clearance. One of the escorting aeroplanes can be seen above the middle funnel.*

was the most beautiful sunset as we steamed west, the ship gently lifting to the Atlantic swell. No maiden voyage could have started under more pleasant conditions.

Long before we reached the other side we were met by three aeroplanes which had been ranging out over the Atlantic looking for us. They circled round the ship, one after the other, and escorted us on our way, and we soon came up with the Nantucket Light Ship. It always seemed strange to me to find the Nantucket and the Ambrose Lights, miles away from anywhere, out of sight of land, but marking the beginning of the channel into the Hudson River and New York. The

Ambrose Channel Light Ship was actually the official end of the transatlantic crossing, and must have been a lonely and often stormy spot for the men that manned it.

As we approached land many eyes were riveted on the horizon. It was a rather misty but beautiful morning, with the promise of a scorching day ahead, and soon away to starboard we could see the long low line of Long Island's silvery-golden beach. We had been at sea for only four days, but even after this short voyage a landfall is exciting. When that landfall is America, and not only America but New York, the world's most dazzling and amazing city, there is every excuse for excitement, and hearts tend to beat a little faster.

We were soon met by the advance party of a veritable navy of boats. There were boats of every description, from quite small boats which found the going a bit rough, to quite large and fast ones. There were naval vessels, coastguard boats, motor boats, sailing boats, speed boats, and when we actually got into the River a number of Hudson River ferry boats, both day boats and night boats, and several Fire Service tenders, all with their hoses in full play like fountains. All these boats had two things in common. They were all packed to the gunwales with people, crammed with human bodies way, way beyond the safety limit, and they all had their whistles and fog horns tied wide open, so that they emitted a continuous note. In every conceivable key and pitch, the resulting barrage of sound was frightful.

Amongst this multitudinous escort the *Queen Mary* proceeded quietly on her way to the Quarantine Station, where she dropped anchor to await Customs, Health and Immigration officials. These duly arrived and cleared her for entry into the Port of New York, upon receipt of which clearance we got our anchor aboard again and proceeded upstream to Pier 90, where yet another special building had been erected for our reception.

Here it was impossible not to smile at the precautions taken for our security, nor to compare American police methods with English. In Southampton there are usually two policemen on duty at the gate into the Docks, two stolid middle-aged English bobbies, and even when the *Queen Mary* arrived for the first time, and the excitement was intense, the guard was not strengthened, and these two appeared to have no difficulty in controlling the crowds. In New York though it was different. At the entrance to Pier 90, and lining the streets on either side,

shoulder to shoulder, were upwards of 600 American cops, all armed, all chewing gum, and all swinging their truncheons. It was like a scene from a Hollywood film.

That evening John Rennie and I were able to go ashore for the first time, and a novel and exciting experience it was. We had difficulty in getting away from the dock due to the crowds, and the still unbroken line of unsmiling policemen. I spoke politely to one, asking permission to cross the road, but he answered not a word, just twirled his truncheon and chewed his gum. We walked along 50th Street as far as Broadway, and then wandered down this great wide street as far as Times Square, where we stood and gawped like any other two tourists at the dazzling multiplicity of neon signs. The largest of these was an enormous rectangle purporting to be the side of an aquarium, in which were swimming a number of exotic, brightly coloured fish. Their tails and fins flapped, and bubbles rose up from their mouths to the surface. What their connection was with the product they were advertising it was difficult to see, for they were promoting chewing gum.

Another sign that fascinated me was high up on a building and represented two acrobats on a high trapeze. The trapezes swung backwards and forwards, one of the acrobats flew across the gap and was caught by the hands of his colleague. This sign perhaps outsmarted itself, for though I remember very clearly what it was like I can't remember what it was promoting.

Broadway was an incredible street, and did not seem to come to life until about 9 o'clock in the evening, but from then on until the early hours it was thronged with people, and life was in full swing. The street lighting was brilliant, and at 1.00 am street photographers were still taking snapshots of passers by.

One of the most noticeable things about Broadway was that of the people you passed in the street—as many were speaking a foreign language as were speaking English. Also there was literally only one topic of conversation—money. When, after several trips to New York I realized that this was invariably so, I found it rather depressing and frightening.

Late at night the streets, and particularly Broadway, were filthy, and there were many strange smells in the air. I understand that the loose paper and garbage were cleared up before dawn, but the chewing gum that had been trodden on to the pavements was there for keeps—except for the odd piece that stuck to the sole of your shoe and which came back aboard with you.

On our first walk ashore, after we had seen some of the sights, and marvelled at the bright lights and the activity all around, John and I decided we were hungry and began to look round for a restaurant. We walked a little way down 42nd Street and found what we took to be a suitable establishment, which only goes to show how green and innocent we were, for in fact it was a 'dime a dance' saloon.

We went down some brightly lit stairs and through the swing doors at the bottom into a dimly lit vestibule. Here we were literally set upon by about eight beautiful young women who fought fairly strenuously for possession of our persons. A general skrimmage took place, and as I was being pulled in about three directions at once I said 'Here, steady on', at which one of the ladies ejaculated 'Christ, a bloody Limey!' Yes, it was that sort of a joint!

When the battle was over we were led into the dance hall proper by our captors. Here the lights were low, the music supplied by a juke box, and we were able to dance with our hostesses—at 10 cents a time. We soon cottoned on to what the game was, namely to extract as much money from us as possible, in the shortest possible time. Ten cents a dance, six dances for 50 cents, but for a dollar the girl was yours for half an hour. The girl that got me, Susie, was a blonde, young and attractive, wearing a green dress. And when I say she was wearing a green dress, I mean just that. I must confess it was very pleasant to dance with her, she had the right sort of contours and knew what she was about. So I paid my dollar fairly willingly.

But this was only the beginning. The girls were paid on commission, and this accounted for the frantic way in which they tried to separate you from your money. They were almost literally fighting for survival, and besides dancing with them there were many things to be bought—drinks, flowers, cigarettes, perfume—on all of which they got a percentage.

After I had paid my dollar Susie dragged me off to the bar for a drink, and here we came up against a rather quaint little bye-law. According to the laws of New York State the girls were not allowed to drink with their escorts, and to get round this the management had provided a ¼ in round rod projecting at right angles from the bar, and we sat on stools on either side of this device. It really wasn't very effective.

I bought her a beer, which tasted very peculiar, some cigarettes, a flower, and some perfume. I don't think she really wanted any of these things, but she was desperate for the money. All these

articles were very expensive and I soon ran out of dollars, so she carted me off to the manager to change a pound note or two. I had a little argument with this gentleman, as he only offered me half the normal rate of exchange, but in the end he gave me something nearer what I considered to be fair. Incidentally, on our next visit to New York, a fortnight later, I happened to see in the paper that this particular man had been shot dead by a dissatisfied customer.

Meanwhile back at the bar, Susie was explaining to me that if I paid $2.50 I could have her exclusive services for the whole evening, and in fact she would be allowed to leave. By this time I was becoming more and more reluctant to part with my good English money, and though she pleaded with me, and promised me that if we went back to her apartment I should not be disappointed, I politely but firmly declined. In the end, in order to convince her, I had to explain that though I found her very attractive I had a girl at home, and was engaged to be married. At which she looked at me wistfully and said 'Gee, I wish I could find a guy as faithful as you!'

I took this to be a great compliment, and hastened back to the safety of the ship, having first said good-bye to John, who was having his own problems in another corner. He arrived back a little later, having had a somewhat similar experience to mine. There was definitely something strange about the beer we had drunk, as we both had bad heads the following morning. There was something even stranger and more terrible about the lives these girls were leading. It was the first time I had ever seen naked greed, and the dreadful power that money can put into the hands of unscrupulous men.

While we were in New York on the maiden voyage the ship was opened to the public, and we were inundated by thousands upon thousands of sightseers and souvenir hunters. The catering department laid up the Cabin Class Restaurant for dinner so that our guests could see what it looked like, but alas, the locusts swept the place bare. Everything went, glass, crockery, cutlery, menus, ashtrays, the lot. I happened to pass two very well dressed, middle aged matrons walking on the Sun Deck, just as one was saying to the other, 'Look what I got!' And she fished in her handbag and brought out a tablespoon.

Our stay in New York only lasted two days but it was a relief to get back to sea again, to relative peace and sanity. The pace of life ashore was very much faster and noisier than we were used to, and though to be English at this time, and a member of the *Queen Mary*'s crew, brought

A more sober arrival in New York. (NB This picture, though typical of normal arrivals, was taken post-war) (University Archives, University of Liverpool).

Above *The Ocean Dock is above the complex in the foreground and is entered from the left. Here Sir Edgar Britten demonstrated the ship's manoeuvrability on the return from the middle voyage* (Southampton City Archives).

Below *Pier 90, New York City, our American berth* (University Archives, University of Liverpool).

many flattering perks, there was something a little spurious and superficial about the whole thing, and it was nice when it stopped.

The voyage back to Europe culminated in another great reception in Southampton, where all the Cunard directors and a huge crowd were assembled round the Ocean Dock. Our Skipper, and Commodore of the Cunard Fleet, Sir Edgar Britten, was guilty of showing off a little when he reached the dock. The usual six tugs came out to meet us, but he waved them aside and turned into the Ocean Dock, almost a right-angled turn, without their help. Once in the dock, which did not look any too large when the *Queen Mary* was in it, he went full speed astern and brought the ship to a standstill in a great confusion of water only feet away from the end of the dock. I think many sightseers who were stationed at this point thought that either the ship was going to continue on up into the High Street, or that they were about to be drowned in the tidal wave she caused. It was an impressive demonstration of her manoeuvrability.

The mind blanches at the thought of the damage she would have caused had he not been able to stop her, for an 80,000 ton displacement ship travelling at about 15 knots carries a tremendous amount of momentum. On one occasion when docking in New York, many moons later, the *Queen Mary* leaned against the Pier 90 building. She was moving imperceptibly at the time, with three tugs trying to control her, and there was no impact. Her overhanging bow just leaned against the building oh, so gently, but where she touched it the building crumbled as if it had been made of paper.

After New York, Southampton seemed very sleepy and peaceful. The crowds which came to see us were as big as in America, but were somehow different. Perhaps the difference lay in that the dock gates were still manned by the same two comfortable, middle-aged English bobbies, and there was not a truncheon, a revolver, nor a stick of chewing gum to be seen anywhere.

Chapter 8

Passengers

In an organization as large and complex as the *Queen Mary*, which ran pretty smoothly and efficiently, it was relatively easy to forget our *raison d'être*—the passengers. In fact, in some ways the passengers were a bit of a nuisance. As far as the engine room was concerned it made no difference whether the ship was carrying passengers or not, and our work was so remote from them that it was quite possible to ignore them. And, of course, the economics of running such an expensive ship was a matter on which the majority of the engineers were blissfully ignorant.

The Chief Engineer was naturally responsible for, and concerned about, his engine room costs, and particularly the fuel bill, which was said to amount to around £50,000 per trip. One day out on deck, when the ship's wake showed that the helmsman was steering a rather erratic and zig-zag course, I heard him complain that if only the bridge would go straight to New York we would travel half the distance and his fuel bill would be considerably less.

The total cost of keeping the *Queen Mary* in service, when you consider not only the day to day running costs, but the cost of the land-based organization at each end, lay-up and engineering costs, etc, etc, must have been astronomical, and the passengers were the only source of that vital commodity, money, with which this outlay could be met. Inflation over the last fifty years has played such havoc with our economic life, and devalued sterling to such an extent, that it is difficult to make valid comparisons, but it is still something of a surprise to find that even in a luxury liner the fares were so low.

The basic Cabin Class fare (return) was £110, Tourist Class £56, and Third Class £37 10s 0d,

sums that today seem ridiculous. But when you consider that she could carry a total of 2,000 passengers it becomes apparent that when running full the income for a round trip could be between £140,000 and £150,000. Multiply this by approximately 25 trips per annum and it is clear that the income was high and that the ship must have been a very profitable venture.

There were many reasons why people chose to travel in the *Queen Mary*. She was new and a 'Royal' ship, she was British, the largest ship in the world, and she was believed to be the fastest. The publicity campaign preceding her going into service had been very cleverly conducted, and to anyone who had to cross the Atlantic there was considerable snob value in travelling in the *Queen Mary*.

The passengers she attracted were many and varied, and it was unkind, and in the majority of cases untrue, to say that they had more money than sense. But money there was in plenty, as a specimen page from the Cabin Class passenger list of 1 July 1936 will indicate. There was a preponderance of Americans, as was perhaps to be expected, and we carried many Hollywood film stars and film producers, as well as bankers, industrialists, and many other types of business tycoon.

What the English lacked in quantity they perhaps made up for in quality, for we were patronized by many members of the aristocracy, diplomats, and wealthy business men. European nobility also, and even royalty, were good customers, King Zog of Albania and his three beautiful sisters—known as 'the Zoglets'—being frequent travellers.

Rules for the engineer officers concerning fraternizing with the passengers were unwritten

Right and below *Typical Cabin Class passenger list,
produced each voyage in our own printing shop.*

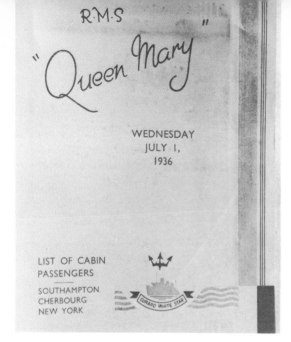

R.M.S

"Queen Mary"

WEDNESDAY
JULY 1,
1936

LIST OF CABIN
PASSENGERS
———
SOUTHAMPTON
CHERBOURG
NEW YORK

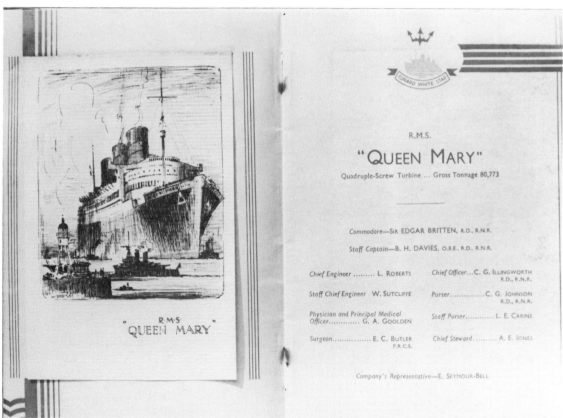

R·M·S
"QUEEN MARY"

R.M.S.

"QUEEN MARY"

Quadruple-Screw Turbine ... Gross Tonnage 80,773

Commodore—Sir EDGAR BRITTEN, R.D., R.N.R.

Staff Captain—B. H. DAVIES, O.B.E., R.D., R.N.R.

Chief Engineer .... L. ROBERTS	Chief Officer...C. G. ILLINGWORTH R.D., R.N.R.
Staff Chief Engineer W. SUTCLIFFE	Purser..............C. G. JOHNSON R.D., R.N.R.
Physician and Principal Medical Officer............ G. A. GOOLDEN	Staff Purser............ L. E. CARINE
Surgeon................ E. C. BUTLER F.R.C.S.	Chief Steward .... A. E. JONES

Company's Representative—E. SEYMOUR-BELL

but fairly strict. There were so many of us compared to the comparatively few pursers and deck officers that we were not encouraged to mix freely with passengers, and could not attend dances, etc. We were of course allowed to use the passenger decks, providing we were correctly dressed in our No 1 uniforms, and when on deck were expected to speak when spoken to, and to be helpful and polite. This stipulation about wearing uniform and looking smart was possibly a

wise rule, since some of us did have a tendency to be rather scruffy, and when you spend so much of your time in the engine rooms there is a great temptation not to shave.

But despite embargoes, unofficial contacts were from time to time made, and some of the young bloods among the engineer officers managed fleeting romances. Fortunately the five-day voyage was generally too short for anything serious to develop. One engineer nearly ruined his career with the Cunard company through this type of indiscretion. He made friends with a girl the first night out, and the next night arranged to meet her again. To avoid being too conspicuous he changed into civilian dress, but as he left his cabin had the misfortune to run into Mr Swanson, one of the Senior Second Engineers. With commendable presence of mind he walked straight on and Swanson let him go. To be wearing civvies during a voyage was a serious matter—worse than not dressing for dinner—and later he received a reprimand, or as it was usually called, a 'heave'.

Actually the rule about wearing uniform applied fairly rigidly in our own ward room and mess room, where it was strictly *de rigueur* to dress for dinner. I found this out to my cost one day when, having fallen asleep in the afternoon, I had no time to change and appeared for dinner in my patrol suit. No one asked me to go and change, but the atmosphere was such that I never did it again.

Each night there was an entertainment of some sort for the passengers, and the officers were allowed to attend these. On one or two evenings a film was shown, and these were always good ones, many of them pre-general release. We also on occasion had the chance of seeing some of the old classics if these were requested by passengers, and, for example, we always knew when Lady Yuill was travelling in the ship because she invariably brought with her a film entitled '*The Turn of the Tide*', the story of a feud between two families of fishermen on the Yorkshire coast, and without exception the finest film I have ever seen.

When show business celebrities travelled in the ship they were sometimes prevailed upon to entertain the passengers, and I well remember Lily Pons, the 'pocket prima donna' singing during a storm when the ship was rolling badly. A rope was rigged right across the stage and she stood clutching this as she sang; a marvellous performance this, and one which many singers would have refused to contemplate. And I shall never forget another occasion when Gracie Fields held a packed audience absolutely spellbound for over two hours. She must have sung almost every song she knew, and such was her art that she had us crying as well as laughing.

Specimen page from a Cabin Class passenger list.

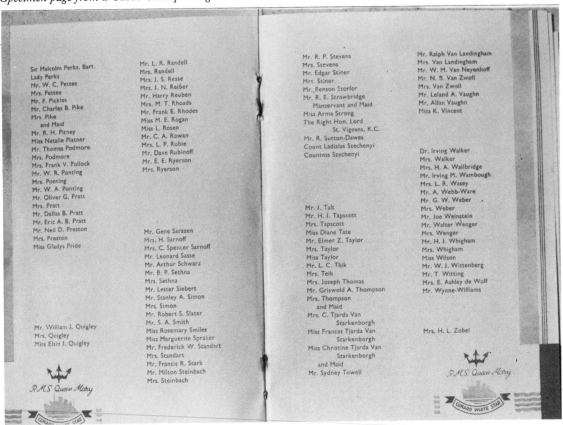

Right *Page One of the Wine List.*

The selection of wines, and especially those intended for consumption on shipboard, calls for the nicest judgment and experience. Ocean travellers are essentially cosmopolitan in their tastes, and in catering for their requirements the Cunard White Star has endeavoured to place on board their ships an assortment of wines of the highest excellence.

Their long experience has been ably assisted by the best expert skill, with the result that the wines listed are of irreproachable quality.

The same high standard is also maintained in spirits, liqueurs and mineral waters; and the cigars and cigarettes are the best known brands and most carefully selected.

The wine which perhaps calls for the most discrimination is champagne, and the Company has hitherto listed only those of English cuvée, which connoisseurs will agree are unsurpassed.

To meet the demand of such passengers who prefer the champagne obtainable on the continent, which is lighter in body, a small selection is now offered.

Cunard White Star

Below *Champagnes at ridiculous prices.*
Below right *A left hand page listing White Burgundies to Moselle.*

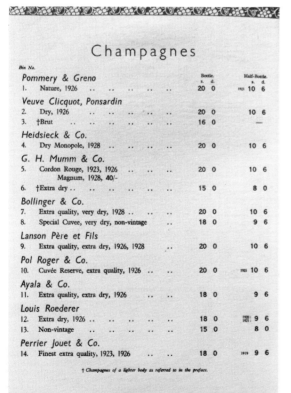

Champagnes

Bin No.			Bottle. s. d.	Half-Bottle. s. d.
Pommery & Greno				
1.	Nature, 1926		20 0	1925 10 6
Veuve Clicquot, Ponsardin				
2.	Dry, 1926		20 0	10 6
3.	†Brut		16 0	—
Heidsieck & Co.				
4.	Dry Monopole, 1928		20 0	10 6
G. H. Mumm & Co.				
5.	Cordon Rouge, 1923, 1926 Magnum, 1928, 40/-		20 0	10 6
6.	†Extra dry		15 0	8 0
Bollinger & Co.				
7.	Extra quality, very dry, 1928		20 0	10 6
8.	Special Cuvee, very dry, non-vintage		18 0	9 6
Lanson Père et Fils				
9.	Extra quality, extra dry, 1926, 1928		20 0	10 6
Pol Roger & Co.				
10.	Cuvée Reserve, extra quality, 1926		20 0	1925 10 6
Ayala & Co.				
11.	Extra quality, extra dry, 1926		18 0	9 6
Louis Roederer				
12.	Extra dry, 1926		18 0	1928 1921 9 6
13.	Non-vintage		15 0	8 0
Perrier Jouet & Co.				
14.	Finest extra quality, 1923, 1926		18 0	1919 9 6

† Champagnes of a lighter body as referred to in the preface.

Burgundy (White)

Bin No.		Vintage.	Bottle. s. d.	Half-Bottle. s. d.
56.	Montrachet Batard	1921	8 6	4 6
57.	Meursault	1923	6 6	3 6
58.	Chablis	1928	4 6	1923 2 6

Empire Wines

		Vintage.	Bottle. s. d.	Half-Bottle. s. d.
59.	Emu	—	4 6	2 6
60.	Chablis, Royal	—	4 6	2 6

Rhine Still Wines

		Vintage.	Bottle. s. d.	Half-Bottle. s. d.
61.	Liebfraumilch Auslese (*Sichel*)	1929	8 0	1923 4 6
62.	Liebfraumilch Nibelungen Krone (*Langenbach*)	1929, 1934	7 6	4 0
63.	Liebfraumilch, Hanns Christof Wein (*Deinhard*)	1925, 1929	7 0	4 0
64.	Deidesheimer Hofstuck	1929	8 0	4 6
65.	Johannisberger Auslese (*Langenbach*)	1929, 1933	7 6	4 0
66.	Forster Auslese (*Julius Kayser*)	1925	7 0	1923 4 0
67.	Rauenthaler (*Deinhard*)	1921	—	3 6
68.	Rudesheimer Superior (*Deinhard*)	—	5 0	2 9
69.	Niersteiner Superior (*Deinhard*)	—	4 6	2 6

Moselle Still Wines

		Vintage.	Bottle. s. d.	Half-Bottle. s. d.
70.	Berncasteler Auslese Gold Label (*Sichel*)	1933	10 0	5 6
71.	Graacher Munslay, Auslese (*Langenbach*)	1929, 1934	11 0	6 0
72.	Piesporter Gold Im Goldtropfchen (*Julius Kayser*)	1926	10 0	5 6
73.	Berncasteler Estate White and Gold Label (*Deinhard*)	—	6 0	3 6
74.	Zeltingen Superior (*Deinhard*)	—	4 6	2 6

Rhine and Moselle Sparkling Wines

Bin No.		Bottle. s. d.	Half-Bottle. s. d.
75.	Sparkling Hock	10 0	5 6
76.	Sparkling Moselle	10 0	5 6

Italian Wines (Red)

		Half-Flask. s. d.	Qtr.-Flask. s. d.
77.	Chianti Ruffino	4 6	2 6
78.	Old Red Antinori	4 0	2 3

Port

		Per Glass. d.
79.	Dow's Royal Dry	10
80.	Cockburn's Special Vintage Character	10
81.	Graham's Six Grapes	8
	Specially selected for Cunard White Star Ltd.	
82.	Hunt's Medium Tawny (very old)	8
	Specially selected for Cunard White Star Ltd.	

Sherry

		Per Glass. s. d.
83.	Harvey's Bristol Cream ..	1 6
84.	Rare Old Sherry (R. & H. Fair) ..	1 3
85.	Dry Sack (Williams & Humbert)	10
86.	Sandeman's ***** Finest Old Pale Dry ..	9
87.	Maxwell's Amontillado ..	9
88.	Brown Sherry (Mendoza's, 1863) ..	9
89.	Gonzalez Vino de Pasto ..	8
90.	Pale Dry Royal Amontillado (Gonzalez Byass & Co.)	8
91.	Golden Amoroso (Gonzalez Byass & Co.)	8

Madeira

Bin No.		Per Glass. d.
92.	Fine Old Pale Dry	8

Liqueurs

	Per Liqueur Glass. d.
Chartreuse, Yellow	10
Chartreuse, Green	10
Benedictine	10
Grand Marnier	10
Crème de Menthe, Green (Cusenier) ..	10
Crème de Menthe, White (Marie Brizard & Rogers) ..	10
Cointreau	10
Kümmel	10
Curaçao, Green Dry	10
Curaçao, Triple Dry	10
Cherry Brandy	10
Maraschino (Cusenier)	10
Crème de Cacao (Cusenier)	10
Peach Brandy	10
Apry Apricot Brandy (Marie Brizard & Rogers) ..	10
Drambuie	10
Hawker's Pedlar Brand Sloe Gin	10
Vodka	10
Calvados	10

Cognac

	Per Liqueur Glass. s. d.
Gautier Frères (Grand Fine Champagne), 70 years old	2 0
Bisquit Dubouché, 1865	2 0
Denis Mounie, 1865	1 9
Hennessy's X.O.	1 6
Martell's Cordon Bleu	1 3
Hines' V.V.S.O.P.	1 0

Cognac—continued

	Per Glass. s. d.
Hennessy's ***	1 3
Martell's ***	1 3
Remy Martin ***	1 3
Courvoisier ***	1 0
Otard's ***	1 0
Hines' ***	1 0
Otard's Flasks, ***, 3 6 each	—
Augier Frères, 25 years old	1 6

Whisky

	Per Glass. s. d.
CUNARD WHITE STAR BLEND (Yellow Label) (Bottled by Cunard White Star Ltd.)	10
(12 years old, specially selected and blended) (Green Label) (Bottled by Distillers Co.)	
King's Ransom (W. Whiteley & Co.)	1 0
Black Label (Johnnie Walker) ..	11
Half-bottle Flask, 6 6 each	
Victoria Vat (J. Dewar & Sons)	11
White Horse (W. H. Distillers Ltd.) ..	10
Large Flask, 6 -; Small Flask, 3 - each	
Black and White (Buchanan's Ltd.) ..	10
Large Flask, 6 -; Small Flask, 3 - each	
White Label (J. Dewar & Sons) ..	10
Large Flask, 6 -; Small Flask, 3 - each	
Red Label (Johnnie Walker) ..	10
Large Flask, 6 - each	
King George IV, Gold Label (Distillers' Agency Ltd.)	10
Gold Label (John Haig)	10
Vat '69 (W. Sanderson & Sons)	10
Queen Anne (Hill, Thomson & Co.) ..	10
MacKinlay's Liqueur (MacKinlay & Co. Ltd.) ..	10
Bisset's Liqueur (J. Bisset & Co.) ..	10
Long John, Princes Reserve (Long John Distilleries Ltd.) ..	10
Perfection (D. & J. McCallum Ltd.) ..	10
Highland Queen, 10 years old (Macdonald & Muir) ..	10
Highland Cream (Wm. Teacher & Sons Ltd.) ..	10

Whisky—continued

	Per Glass. d.
Best Procurable (Hudson's Bay Company)	10
Gold Label (Bulloch Lade & Co.)	10
Cutty Sark (Berry Bros.)	10
Glenlivet V.O.B. (Churtons Ltd.)	10
Dunville's V.R. Irish (Dunville & Co. Ltd.) ..	10
Irish, 10 years old (J. Jameson & Sons) ..	10
Three Swallows, Irish (J. Power & Sons) ..	10
Old Bushmills *** Irish (The Old Bushmills' Distillery Co. Ltd.) ..	10
Canadian Club (H. Walker & Sons) ..	10
American Bourbon (H. Walker & Sons) ..	10
Lincoln Inn Rye (Distillers' Corporation—Seagrams Ltd.) ..	10
Seagram's Bourbon (Distillers' Corporation—Seagrams Ltd.) ..	10

Gin

	Per Glass. d.
Booth's High and Dry	10
Gordon's London, Dry	10
Gordon's Orange Lemon	10
Nicholson's Old Tom	10
Bols Geneva	10
De Kuyper's	10
Gilbey's	10

Rum

	Per Glass. s. d.
Bacardi	1 3
Charley's Punchbowl	1 0
Myers'	1 0
Jamaica	10

Aperitifs

	Per Glass. s. d.
Amer Picon	1 3
Fernet Branca	1 0
Aalborg Akvavit	10
Gin and Bitters	10
Gin and Vermouth	9
Sherry and Bitters	9
Mixed Vermouth	8
Vermouth, Italian, Martini Rossi	8
Vermouth, French, Noilly Prat	8
Dubonnet	8
Kina Lillet	8

Far left *The following right hand page—Moselles to Sherry.*

Left *Left hand page—Madeira to Cognac.*

Below far left *Right hand page—Cognac to Whisky.*

Below left *Left hand page—Whisky to Aperitifs.*

Right *A selection of cigarettes available on board.*

Cigarettes			Each s. d.
EGYPTIAN—			
Prince de Monaco (*Ed. Laurens*) ..	..	Box of 20	1 8
Melachrino	..	„ 10	10
Abdulla	..	„ 12	1 0
TURKISH—			
No. 12 (*Ed. Laurens*)	..	Box of 25	1 10
Philip Morris	..	„ 10	1 0
Abdulla	..	„ 12	1 3
Pall Mall	..	„ 10	1 0
Savory (Plain Russian)	..	„ 25	1 8

VIRGINIAN—	Flat Tins of 50. s. d.	Packets 20. s. d.	Packets 10. s. d.
Capstan	2 0	—	—
Pall Mall de Luxe ..	2 0	—	—
Craven A	2 0	10	5
De Reszke	2 0	10	5
Gold Flake (Wills') ..	2 0	10	5
Player's Navy Cut (Medium) ..	2 0	10	5
State Express No. 555 ..	2 6	1 0	6
State Express No. 333 ..	2 0	10	5
Kensitas	—	10	5
Du Maurier	—	10	—
Black and White ..	—	—	8
Three Castles	—	1 2	—
Sweet Afton	—	9	—
Escudo	.. Box of 25	1 9	

VARIOUS—			
Spud	.. Box of 20	8	
Kool	„ 20	7	
Camel	„ 20	7	
Lucky Strike	„ 20	7	
Chesterfield	„ 20	7	
Old Gold	„ 20	7	
Philip Morris (English Blend) ..	„ 20	7	

In the daytime there were plenty of amusements for passengers, but the majority seemed to prefer lying out in a deck chair on the Promenade Deck. These chairs were put out every morning complete with mattress, cushions and rug, and were very comfortable. Reading matter was also supplied, and one morning every chair had been provided with a copy of the very latest book to be published—*Gone With the Wind*. This was obviously a publicity stunt, but to see a row of hundreds of chairs all carrying the same book was an impressive sight, and I hope the publicity agent got a satisfactory photograph.

Passengers needed as much exercise as sleep, since there was so much good food available, and drinks in the various bars were ridiculously cheap. I still possess many menus from all three classes in the ship, and the standard of food was unreservedly excellent. The Cabin Class wine list was an expensively produced brochure, but the prices it listed hardly bear looking at these days. However, the relative prices make interesting reading. There were 31 proprietary brands of whisky listed, all except three being priced at 10d a glass. There were seven different gins, also at 10d per glass. Liqueurs were also 10d, but the fourteen Cognacs varied from 1/- to 2/-. Bass, Worthington and other beers were 6d per bottle, and lager 7d to 10d. Cigarettes were 10d for 20, or 2/- for a flat tin of fifty. Cigars were upwards of 8d, the most expensive being Corona Coronas, *Queen Mary* Selection No 6 at 7/6d each. Wines followed the same pattern. A large number of Champagnes were carried, the most expensive—Pommery & Greno '26, Pol Roger '26, Heidsieck '28 or Bollinger '28—being priced at 20/- per bottle. Gevrey Chambertin was 7/6d a bottle, and so was a Chateau bottled Claret. Chablis, Niersteiner and Chianti were all 4/6d. Sherry was 8d a glass.

Accustomed as we are to inflation, and to the great con trick that decimalized our currency and sent prices soaring overnight, these figures still seem almost unbelievable, and they must of course be assessed against the value of money at the time, and the scale of wages. I have already commented on the low wages paid to stewards, and the fact that the level of tipping was high, so that the latter provided their principal source of income. As an example of this, the Verandah Grill barman told me that following the maiden voyage he was able to bank a sum of over £200, and he had only been standing behind a bar dispensing drinks. He also told me of a bell-boy, whose first trip to sea it was, whose haul was £60.

Among the interesting passengers I met was a young American about my own age, though this was the only point of similarity between us, for I was thin and he was very fat. Also, I was poor and he was immensely rich, so rich in fact that he was spending his life travelling around in luxury liners, having nothing better to do. He crossed with us several times and had already been round the world thirteen times. The thing I remembered most about him was his performance in the swimming pool. He was not an outstanding swimmer yet he was so fat that he found it impossible to sink, and it was an extraordinary sight to see him lying about in the water, for all the world like some great balloon. For all his wealth, however, his life was aimless, and his money was doing no one any good, least of all himself.

Many of the Americans we carried were of course tourists, either on their way to 'do' Europe, or on their way back having 'done' it. The attitude of some of them to their holiday was appalling; they were not really interested in what they were going to see, but merely wanted to visit as many places as possible so that they could boast about it when they got back home. The motivation of these poor souls was simply to keep up with the Jones's, or rather to outdo the Jones's, but as far as Cunard White Star was concerned it was very good for business.

Travelling to the United States, even in the luxury of the *Queen Mary*, did not absolve passengers from complying with the rather complicated immigration regulations regarding baggage, US Customs, and—if you were a temporary visitor—recovery of US Head Tax, which everyone entering the States had to pay. There were so many notices to be brought to the attention of travellers that Cunard incorporated these in a booklet together with general information about the ship. The following is an extract from these notices:

'*Recovery of US Head Tax*. Passengers who desire to claim refund of Head Tax are required to comply with the following—

'**1** Temporary visitors to the United States should state in Question 24 on the US Declaration Form, which should be completed at the time of booking, that they intend to leave the United States within a period of 60 days from the date of entry. *NOTE*—If a passenger states on the Declaration Form that the intended stay is to be in excess of 60 days, and later through unforeseen circumstances leaves within the prescribed period, United States law stipulates that Head Tax is not recoverable.

'**2** Application should be made to the Purser of the Westbound steamer for receipt covering the United States Head Tax paid. This is necessary to facilitate refund of the Head Tax after passengers have left the United States.

'**3** Passengers should apply to the United States Immigration Inspector at the port of arrival for Head Tax Transit Certificate (United States Form 514) without which form no refund of Head Tax will be considered by the United States Immigration Authorities, even though passengers should leave the United States within 60 days and would otherwise be entitled to refund of the Head Tax under existing United States law.

'**4** Refund of Head Tax will only be made by the United States Authorities when completed Forms 514 are filed with them within a period of 120 days from the date of entry into the United States as shewn on the top right-hand corner of the United States Form 514. No application for refund of Head Tax will be considered by the United States Authorities after the expiry of such period. Refund of Head Tax is subject to strict compliance with the above procedure.'

As can be seen from the above, entry into the United States was not without its problems, and anyone thinking that in leaving Europe they were leaving bureaucracy behind was due for a disappointment. The regulations continue:

'*Automobiles* In order to facilitate Customs clearance uncrated automobiles must be included on the US Declaration Form.

'*Baggage* Questions relating to Baggage should be referred to the Purser or ship's Baggage Master.

'*US Customs* All passengers are required to make a declaration of personal baggage for the US Customs authorities at New York. Blank declaration forms are obtainable from the Purser. Returning residents of the United States must declare all articles acquired abroad but wearing apparel and personal effects taken overseas from the US in the first case are entitled to be passed free of duty on return. An exemption of $100.00 of purchases is allowed each returning resident, subject to certain conditions which will be detailed by the Customs officer. Visitors may take in free of duty wearing apparel and personal effects not intended for sale, but must declare all articles not included in this category. Severe penalties are imposed upon persons who make false declarations as to value, ownership or use of articles or who attempt to bribe or recompense a Customs officer.

'*Customs examination* All articles liable to Customs duty must be declared. Any passenger who is in doubt should see the Purser or Baggage Master who will provide the latest information available. On arrival baggage will be grouped alphabetically in Customs shed for examination. To help the passing and claiming of baggage passengers should have one of the Company's labels, bearing the initial letter of their surname, affixed to each piece. The bedroom stewards have a supply of these labels and will affix them prior to landing. It is for passengers themselves to see that all their baggage is passed by the Customs authorities on landing, and they are specially requested to claim their baggage before leaving the Customs shed, otherwise delay and extra charges for carriage will be incurred in forwarding to destination any baggage not accompanying passengers directly from the ship.

'*Checking baggage on arrival at New York* Facilities are available whereby passengers may arrange with the ship's Baggage Master for the transfer of their baggage from the Company's pier in New York to any point in Greater New York, Jersey City and Hoboken, including railroad terminals, hotels, residences, express companies or warehouses. Passengers are thus relieved of this detail after disembarking. Rates and further information regarding this service can be obtained at the Purser's Office.

'*Baggage in bond* Passengers en route to destinations outside the USA may have their checked baggage forwarded 'In Bond' to a frontier point under Customs manifest without examination of the contents by a Customs officer at New York. The Purser or Baggage Master will be pleased to supply information.

'*Baggage insurance* Passengers are recommended to insure their baggage as the Company's liability is strictly limited in accordance with the terms of the passage contract. Baggage insurance carrying world-wide cover can be arranged through the Purser's office.

'*Banking, foreign money exchange* A branch of the Midland Bank is available on board the ship where passengers wishing to exchange money, or transact other banking business will receive every attention.

'*Catering* Passengers are invited to advise the Restaurant Manager or Head Waiter of their preference in the matter of diet and cooking and they can be assured of every attention to their wishes. Cooks of various nationalities are included in the kitchen personnel. It is suggested that passengers order their meals in advance, and

the aforementioned officials will readily assist passengers in making their choice.

'*Changes in accommodation* The Purser alone is authorised to make changes in accommodation and may only do so on payment of any difference in fare which may be required according to the Company's current tariffs.

'*Complaints* Passengers entertaining any cause for complaint are requested to communicate particulars to a responsible officer in the ship, so that an opportunity may be afforded to adjust matters.

'*Deck chairs, cushions and rugs* are available for hire and can be obtained through the Deck Steward at the price of 5/- each article. (Each rug is contained in a sealed envelope and bears a serial number worked into the material, thus enabling passengers to identify their own rugs.)

'*Dogs* Passengers are notified that dogs should be handed over to the care of the livestock attendant and that they are not allowed in public rooms or on the passenger decks. Deck space over 80 feet in length is provided for the exercise of animals on the Sun Deck, where kennels and accommodation for 26 dogs are also located.

'*Fire precautions* Passengers are specially requested to exercise care in disposing of cigar and cigarette ends and matches and to make use of the receptacles provided for the purpose in the different parts of the ship, in view of the serious consequences which can arise from carelessness in this respect. Throwing lighted cigarettes overboard should also be avoided.

'*Fire and lifeboat stations* Passengers are earnestly requested to acquaint themselves with the notice in the staterooms regarding lifeboat and fire stations. The Captain specially appeals to passengers to assist him by promptly mustering at their appointed stations at all times when passenger boat stations muster is being held. Only by immediate attendance at this important muster can passengers obtain the necessary instructions which are so vital to the well-being of all on board. The co-operation of every passenger is earnestly desired.

'*Importation of liquor* A considerable quantity of Liquor imported in the baggage of passengers is purchased 'in bond' at a price below the regular market value in the country of purchase and for that reason attention is called to the fact by the Collector, US Customs Service, that the above market value must be ascertained and declared by the passenger instead of the price actually paid.

'*Landing arrangements* The Purser will furnish passengers with a small card, detailing the landing arrangements, before arrival. It is necessary that passengers present their landing cards, together with passports, to the Immigration Inspector for endorsement before leaving the ship.

'*Mail* Passengers who may expect letters, postal packages, etc, should apply at the mail office, and also leave their addresses so that any mail, etc, arriving after they have landed, can be re-directed.

'*Passage tickets* Passengers are requested to hand their passage tickets to their bedroom stewards as soon as possible after embarkation.

'*Payments* Passengers should obtain a receipt of the Company's form for any payment made on board for additional passage money, rugs, chairs, excess baggage, etc.

'*Portholes* As it is dangerous for passengers to handle the ports they are requested to ask the bedroom steward to open and close the ports in the staterooms as may be desired.

'*Professional gamblers* are reported as frequently travelling in Atlantic ships and passengers are warned to take precautions accordingly.

'*Radio Telephone service* Passengers can speak from the ship to Great Britain, France, Germany, Spain, Holland, Belgium, Sweden, Switzerland, Denmark, Austria, and to the United States and Canada.

	Rates per call of three minutes or less	Each extra minute
Great Britain	£3 12s 0d	£1 4s 0d
New York	$18.00	$6.00

'The rate to Great Britain is £1 16s 0d (three minutes) plus 12/- each extra minute, when the ship is within 500 miles of Great Britain, and $9 (three minutes) plus $3 each extra minute, to New York when the ship is within 500 miles of the American coast. Rates to other places are also reduced whilst the vessel is within the zones indicated. A Secrecy Device is used which renders a telephone conversation unintelligible to any unauthorised person.

'*Radio and cable messages* Information and rates will be supplied by the Radio Office.

'*Radio receivers and electrical apparatus* Private radio receivers or other electrical apparatus must not be operated or connected to the ship's electrical supply circuits without official approval, applications for which should be made to the Purser. Passengers using loud-speakers are requested to avoid disturbing their fellow passengers.

'*Return accommodation* For the convenience of those passengers who may be returning from Canada or the United States to Europe and who have not yet made the necessary arrangements the Purser will be pleased to radio for any accommodation required. This will enable passengers to complete their arrangements before leaving the ship and will consequently save them time and trouble after landing.

'*Rotarians* travelling by this ship are invited to inspect the Rotary Register at the Purser's office and subscribe their names. The Purser will be glad, providing circumstances permit, to arrange an informal meeting during the voyage.

'*Special notice for round trip passengers* All passengers holding return tickets are requested to communicate with the most convenient Company's office, if possible at least a week in advance of their intended sailing from the United States or Canada, so that the necessary formalities may be arranged in connection with their passage.

'If for any reason the holder of a return ticket should be unable to travel by the sailing shown thereon, immediate advice should be given to the nearest Company's office, so that any accommodation can be released and new reservation made in sailing selected.

'*Departure from America—US Sailing Permit* All passengers other than US citizens are required to obtain a sailing permit or income tax clearance prior to departure from the United States. This document can be obtained without difficulty from the Collector of Internal Revenue in each district, or on personal application, with passport and passage ticket a day or two before sailing, at Room 131, US Custom House, foot of Broadway, New York City.

'*Stewards speaking foreign languages* Stewards speaking a number of European languages are available for the convenience of passengers and may be identified by the badge worn on the lapel of their coat bearing the flag of the country the language of which they speak.

'*Taxicabs* can be hired at the New York piers. It is suggested to passengers for their own protection that Terminal Cabs, which come within the pier gates, afford comfort and protection for passengers and their baggage at reasonable rates.

'*The Physician and Surgeon* are authorised to make customary charges for their services, subject to the approval of the Captain.

'*Registered nurses* are on board, whose services are available as necessary under the direction of the ship's medical officers.

'*Turkish and electric baths* The baths are open for the use of gentlemen and ladies during the following hours:

Gentlemen	Ladies
7.00 am to 10.00 am	10.00 am to 2.30 pm
2.30 pm to 7.30 pm	

'*Valeting Service* A clothes pressing room, in charge of an expert attendant, is provided and work of this kind will be carried out for passengers at the following charges:

Gentlemen	s	d
Lounge and dress suits	4	0
Lounge and dress coats	2	0
Trousers and breeches	2	0
Overcoats—heavy	4	0
Overcoats—light	3	0

Ladies	s	d
Suits, costumes, coats, frocks or dresses	4	0
Dress coats and plain coats	4	0
Skirts	2	0

Special charges for—
Garments—velvet, silk or pleated fancy dress, blouses and scarves.

'*Valuables* For the convenience of passengers having with them valuables, or articles of jewellery, a Safe Deposit is installed, adjacent to the Purser's office on A-Deck. The Safe Deposit contains nearly 300 compartments and passengers desiring to avail of this facility should make request to the Purser who will supply a key. Passengers are asked to exercise care to avoid mislaying the key handed to them as in the case of loss, delay may result in obtaining access to the contents of the compartments allotted. Keys are to be returned to the Purser on the completion of the voyage.

'The Company can accept no liability as to the contents placed in a compartment of the Safe Deposit and passengers are advised to protect themselves by insurance. In their own interest passengers are advised not to leave articles of value lying about.

'*Verandah Grill* is located on Sun Deck. Meals will be served during the hours of 12 noon to 3 pm, 7 pm to 10 pm. A charge of 5/- is made to each passenger occupying a seat at a table during these hours.'

From the above it is apparent that crossing the Atlantic was not just a simple matter of buying a ticket and booking a cabin. Fortunately members of the crew were not troubled with all these various forms, and we did not even have to have a passport. All we were provided with was a single document in booklet form, very similar in size and colour to a British passport. This was deposited in the engineers' office aboard the ship and every so often was stamped with a rubber stamp to say that our conduct had been good.

Chapter 9

Running the ship

Once the maiden voyage was over, and the excitement had died down, we soon got into a fortnightly routine of regular voyages, one trip becoming very like another. Depending on the tide we would normally leave Southampton early on Wednesday morning and cross to Cherbourg to embark passengers from Europe. We never stayed more than a few hours in Cherbourg, and were usually on our way westwards by late afternoon. Given reasonable weather conditions the Ambrose Light Vessel would be reached early on the following Monday morning, and soon after breakfast time we would be tied up in our berth at Pier 90 in New York City.

We would leave New York again on Wednesday, arriving Cherbourg early on Monday. Though our stay in Cherbourg was short, this call meant that we were always later in arriving home in Southampton than in arriving in New York on the alternate Mondays, a fact that did not please the family men among the crew, whose homes were in Southampton. If we were delayed on the eastward crossing by fog or bad weather we could quite easily miss the tide up Southampton Water and have to wait for several hours. There were occasions when we were as much as 24 hours late, not arriving in Southampton until Tuesday afternoon. These were occasions we all dreaded for we still had to leave again on Wednesday morning to maintain the scheduled service, and it was just too bad if maintenance work had to be done while we were in port. The Chief Superintendent Engineer had been quite right when he said the *Queen Mary* would be a difficult ship to run. She was.

Even when we were keeping to our scheduled times she was far from easy on the crew, due

principally to her speed. New York time is five hours behind ours, and as we were doing the westward crossing in 4½ days it meant that each night as we travelled west the clocks had to go back one hour. Each day on the outward journey therefore was 25 hours long. Travelling eastwards of course the reverse applied and the clocks went forward one hour each night, so that every day was only 23 hours long.

The effect that this constant changing in clock time had on your body can perhaps be imagined, and it is no exaggeration to say that it played havoc with your sleep pattern and other bodily functions, especially when travelling east. It was never possible to achieve any bodily rhythm at all.

For example, if you were in the habit of going to bed at, say, 11 o'clock each night, then on the first night out from New York the clock would go forward one hour, so that when the clock said 11 o'clock your body was saying it was still only 10 o'clock. On the second night out at 11 o'clock by the clock your body believed it was really only 9 o'clock, the next night 8 o'clock, then 7 o'clock, and on the night the ship reached Europe 6 o'clock. By this time your body was so completely confused that it would refuse to sleep at all.

Coupled with this was the fact that we worked sea watches of four hours on duty and eight hours off. In other words, if you were on the 4 to 8 watch you worked from 4.00 am to 8.00 am and from 4.00 pm to 8.00 pm. During your eight hours off you had to wash, change, eat, sleep and have your recreation, so that it was never possible to get eight hours uninterrupted sleep. You were therefore perpetually trying to snatch a little sleep at times when your body was

Above *Night departure from Southampton (post-war picture)* (University Archives, University of Liverpool).

Below *The bill for fresh flowers was staggering as they were all changed each trip. The four gardeners we carried were known affectionately as 'flower stranglers'* (University Archives, University of Liverpool).

Electricians, posed rather uncharacteristically for the camera (University Archives, University of Liverpool).

resisting—and dropping off to sleep when it was time to get up and go on watch. Getting up at 3.30 am was sometimes particularly trying.

Actually, in many ways the 4 to 8 was the best watch of all. Once you had got over the physical strain of getting up so early you came off watch at 8.00 am ready for breakfast, which for this watch was at 9.00 am. You ate this in peace and comfort and under no pressures, the other watches and day workers having breakfasted earlier. You then had the best part of the day at your disposal until 4.00 pm though some of this time had to be spent in sleep. At 8.00 pm you were free again for a leisurely dinner at 9 o'clock, and then to bed until 3.30 am.

The 8 to 12 watch meant that you breakfasted at 7.15 am, lunched at 1.00 pm, and dined at 7.00 pm. On this watch most of your sleep could be taken between, say, 12.30 am and 6.30 am. The third watch, from 12 to 4, was a curious one, in that if you went to bed on coming off watch at 4 am you stood a good chance of missing your

breakfast. This was not a good thing to do as you were bound to miss your lunch too, though at least you could make up for things at dinner time.

All three watches had their different characteristics, and in order to prevent anyone getting into a rut we had to change watches every trip. That is, having done one round voyage on the 4 to 8 watch, the next one would be on the 8 to 12 watch, and the next one on the 12 to 4; and so on.

These were basic hours—four on and eight off—but there were many extras. When leaving or arriving in port, or in fog, the watch was always doubled, which meant that if you were on the 4 to 8 watch, and it was foggy at 8 o'clock, you stayed on duty for another four hours, on standby. The stand-by watch was well named, as there was absolutely nothing for you to do but just stand there, and try to keep awake. . . The North Atlantic is notorious for fog, and the *Queen Mary* was arriving at or leaving port every few days, so that there were plenty of stand-by watches, and these were not popular! It must be remembered too that there was no such thing as a five-day week, or a weekend break. No, you worked seven days a week, and if you were at sea it made no difference if it was Sunday, or Easter Monday, or Christmas Day, the ship had to be run.

The work itself was not onerous when you were a junior on switchboard duty, for there was nothing to do unless and until something went wrong. In fact this was the big snag about the job—there was no mental activity at all—and the result was boredom. With hindsight I can see now that perhaps I should have requested permission to take service manuals and drawings of some of the electrical plant down below for study during the long drawn-out four hours of a watch, but this never occurred to me at the time, and indeed might well have been vetoed.

Instead, I introduced my own mental activity and started to write—mainly short stories and poetry, though it was also a good opportunity for writing letters. As a change I also started designing houses and bungalows, and in addition learned—in a very amateurish way—various types of lettering, particularly Old English, my *pièce de resistance* being an illuminated copy of *Greensleeves*. On the switchboard platform there was a large desk which was ideal for this work, and the lighting was excellent. The desk was also capacious enough to hold all my writing materials on the infrequent visits of a supervisor. Perhaps I was lucky that I was never caught at this extra-mural activity, and managed to dream my way through many a tedious watch.

Down below was a brightly lit, exciting world, with the continuous hum of machinery. The first machinery spaces were situated approximately under the bridge and contained tank rooms and the Water Softening Plant. Forward of these spaces, and below the level of the lowest (H) deck were the general cargo holds, which were surprisingly large.

Aft of the Water Softening Plant was No 1 Boiler Room containing the three double-ended Scotch boilers which supplied steam for the Forward, or Hotel Services, Power Station. Then came Boiler Room No 2, holding six Yarrow boilers, this being the first of four similar boiler rooms supplying steam for the propulsion of the ship. Immediately aft of No 2 Boiler Room was the Hotel Services Generating Station with

Below left *Hotel Services Switchboard in the Forward Turbo-generator Room—similar to the Machinery Supply Board, but controlling only three 1,300 kw BTH generators* (University Archives, University of Liverpool).

Below right *The Scotch boilers in No 1 Boiler Room, supplying steam for the Hotel Services turbo-generators* (University Archives, University of Liverpool).

SECTION AT FRAME 108,
LOOKING FORWARD

SECTION AT FRAME 116,
LOOKING AFT

SECTION AT FRAME 134,
LOOKING FORWARD

ELEVATION

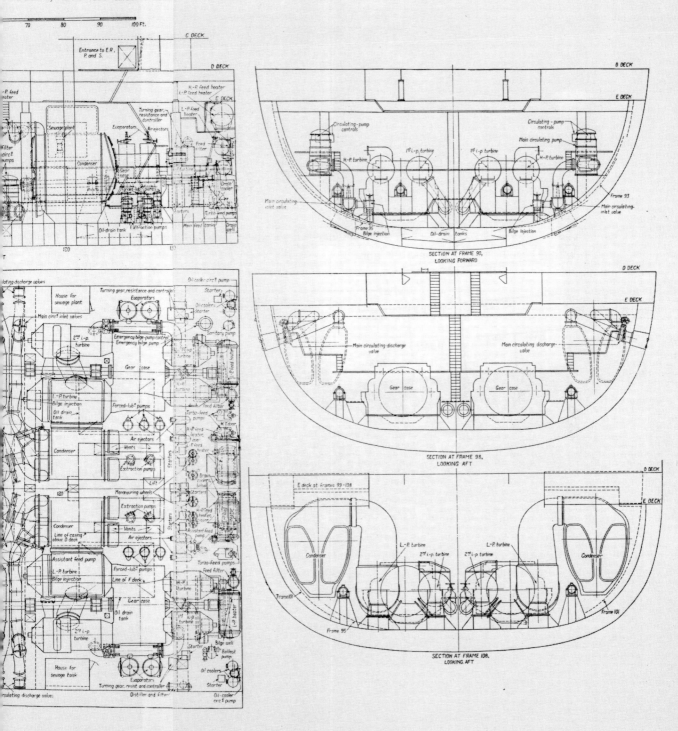

SECTION AT FRAME 90,
LOOKING FORWARD

SECTION AT FRAME 98,
LOOKING AFT

SECTION AT FRAME 108,
LOOKING AFT

Three of the four 1,300 kW BTH turbo-generators in the Machinery Supply Generating Room (University Archives, University of Liverpool).

its three 1,300 kW BTH turbo-generators, the controlling switchboard being mounted on the forward bulkhead above the turbines, so that from the platform you looked down on the machinery being controlled.

Then came Boiler Rooms 3 and 4, each containing six more Yarrow boilers, followed by the other power station which supplied electricity for the main propulsion auxiliaries by means of four more 1,300 kW BTH turbo-generators. Again the switchboard was mounted on the forward bulkhead above the turbines. Aft of this power station was No 5, the last of the four main boiler rooms, and from this room you passed directly into the Forward Engine Room, thence into the After Engine Room, and finally into the shaft tunnels.

To increase the efficiency of the boilers, the

boiler rooms were kept under pressure by means of huge forced draught fans, so that every entrance to the boiler rooms had to be protected by an airlock, which was a small compartment, big enough to hold two men, and with airtight doors in and out. To enter a boiler room you had to open the airlock and step inside, closing and locking the door carefully behind you. You could then open the other door into the pressurized boiler room.

The pressure was only about five inches of water gauge, but this was enough to make your ears pop and some people found it unpleasant. Each boiler room was separated from the next by a water-tight bulkhead, and the doors through these bulkheads were positioned in the middle of the airlocks. The water-tight doors were operated hydraulically by means of a lever on each side of the door, and when they opened or closed a great bell clanged a warning. When passing through one you had to be careful, as there was not much room and the moment you

let go of the handle, the door, which was of very heavy steel construction, would begin to close automatically. Fortunately, they were normally kept open and only closed in fog, so that you only had to cope with the airlock doors. The trickiest of these water-tight doors was between the two engine rooms, as this was a vertical one which descended like a great guillotine when it closed.

The Forward and After engine rooms were quite different in appearance. The forward room housed the two inboard engines which were side by side, and consequently it gave the appearance of being full of machinery. The forward starting platform, which contained the main steam valves, the engine telegraphs and other instruments, was a comparatively small space, whereas in the after engine room, where the engines were driving the two outer shafts, the starting platform was wide and spacious with headroom right up to the engine room skylight.

From the After Engine Room ran the tunnels which carried the shafts from the engines, way

Close up of a 1,300 kW BTH generator (University Archives, University of Liverpool).

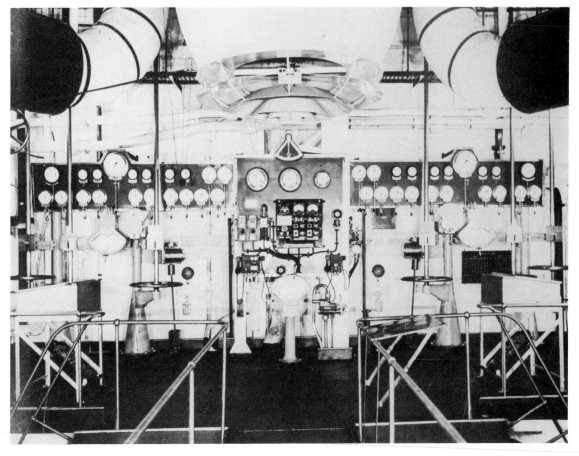

under the ship to the stern. These shafts were supported every few feet in bearings, and a gangway ran down through the tunnels so that these bearings could be inspected, and also the stern glands where the shafts passed out through the ship's bottom into the sea. The tunnels were well lit and very much cooler than the engine rooms, and in very hot weather it was a pleasant change to work down there. The sight of these very long and enormous shafts—2 ft 6 in in diameter—turning away was very impressive, though the tunnels were rather lonely places and you were conscious of being hundreds of feet away from human company.

There were other lonely places in the ship too, such as the Forced Draught Fan Rooms, which housed the huge electrically driven fans which kept the boiler rooms under pressure. These were not well lit and in winter were extremely cold as they sucked down large quantities of fresh air through the ventilators on the top deck. In one storm I had to go down and fit new carbon brushes to one of the motors which had been drenched by an estimated 20 tons of water which had come down the ventilator, and this was a very cold and wet job. This ventilator, incidentally, was situated behind and above the bridge, and must have been about 130 ft above water level.

The loneliest place in which I ever had to work was a little compartment in the forward part of the ship, right away from everyone. This compartment was in the ship's side and housed a patent log, known as the Chernikeef Log after its inventor. Mr Chernikeef was a funny little elderly Russian whom I had the pleasure of meeting on one occasion. He lived in Siberia, which is so remote that he very seldom managed to get home. His description of the train journey he had to take from Moscow to his home town, a jour-

ney that took two weeks night and day, was fascinating!

The Chernikeef Log was operated by a small propeller on the end of a bronze shaft about three feet long, and this propeller was pushed out through a hole in the ship's side where it was rotated by the water to drive a small electric generator. The current generated then recorded speed and distance travelled on an instrument up on the bridge. Every so often this device had to be examined and serviced, and to do this it had to be withdrawn from the ocean. It was pulled back into a housing bolted to the ship's side, and the hole it had come through was sealed off by means of a valve. The log could then be withdrawn from the housing for examination.

Obviously it was important that the valve should be tightly shut before the log was withdrawn from its housing, and in case the electrician who was doing the job made a mistake and let the Atlantic in, he had to climb into the very small compartment in which the log was situated, and seal himself in with a watertight door. Then if he made a mistake and forgot to close the valve the only damage done would be the loss of one electrician.

There were of course many other jobs for the electrician, other than those in the engine rooms, and fortunately the juniors were not kept down below on the switchboards permanently. Besides the large amount of electrical plant used in connection with the propulsion of the ship, there were also many items 'up top' which were equally important. The air-conditioning plant alone was extensive, every cabin in the ship having a supply of fresh air, and there were innumerable small fan rooms spread about the ship from one end to the other. All this plant had to be inspected regularly to ensure satisfactory operation.

There were 21 lifts, most of which were in constant use every day, and in a seaway the stresses and strains on a lift were very much greater than on one in a stationary building. On the forward deck there were several cargo winches, out in the open and frequently wet with salt water. These were only used in port, but when needed it was important that they worked instantly and efficiently. Other deck equipment included the navigation lights, electrically operated whistles, and the lifeboat winches. In the stern of the ship, next to the steering gear compartment, was an emergency generating set, which had to be kept in instant readiness.

All the equipment in the galleys was electrical, and it was vital that this should not break down.

Top left *Two of the main circulating pumps. These pumped sea water into the condensers so that exhausted steam from the turbines could be turned back into water and re-used in the boilers* (University Archives, University of Liverpool).

Top right *Forward Engine Room Starting Platform, controlling the two inboard engines. The horizontal wheels operated the main steam valves to the turbines* (University Archives, University of Liverpool).

Left *After Engine Room Starting Platform, controlling the outboard engines. On 'fog stand-by', or when approaching or entering harbour, this is where I had to stand for four hours, with nothing to do but keep awake, after a four-hour watch on the switchboard* (University Archives, University of Liverpool).

Apart from the many ovens and boiling rings, there was a complete bakery, and literally dozens of pieces of auxiliary equipment such as potato peelers, refrigerators, slicing machines, grills, toasters, water boilers, dish-washing machines, refuse destructors, etc, etc, etc. The printing shop, which dealt with menus, the daily paper, and other notices, was also all electric.

Every one of the several hundred clocks in the ship was altered each night from a master clock, and inevitably some of these gave trouble. There were 30,000 electric lamps in the ship, and though their mortality was not high, lamping up was a regular and frequent job. This was naturally done in the small hours when most passengers were asleep. So that besides the electricians working down below some worked what were called deck watches to look after all this varied equipment, and also of course to look after the passengers, many of whom wanted English type plugs put on to their radios and hair curlers, etc.

We had not crossed the Atlantic many times before we started to have trouble with some of our electric motors. All new machinery is subject to teething troubles, and this had been anticipated, but the principal trouble experienced was most unexpected as it was due to smoke. At the speed the *Queen Mary* travelled a partial vacuum was created at the stern of the ship as she swept along, and the smoke from her funnels was sucked down into this, cascading all over the after decks and into the ventilators which fed air into the engine rooms. The smoke was full of very fine grit besides having a sulphurous smell, and the atmosphere in the engine rooms became gritty too. The grit got on to the copper commutator of some of the electric motors which were fitted with a soft graphite type of carbon brush—these started to score, and within a few weeks we were faced with grooves up to ⅛ in deep. These caused sparking and bad commutation, which led to further wear, and before long we were in big trouble.

Top left *Generator telegraph, installed on the Forward Engine Room Starting Platform and communicating with the Machinery Supply Generator Switchboard. An unnecessary instrument, unpopular with engineers, and consequently little used* (University Archives, University of Liverpool).

Left *The port outer shaft, of 2 ft 6 in diameter, turning at around 200 rpm. The shaft tunnels leading from the engine rooms right aft to the stern glands, were long and lonely* (University Archives, University of Liverpool).

The immediate electrical cure was to fit a different grade of carbon brush, which would not trap the grit, but the long term cure was of course to get rid of the grit, or to stop the smoke descending on the after decks. The latter was more desirable as it was impossible to keep the grit out of your eyes, and there were many complaints from passengers in the Tourist Class.

Several palliatives were tried, and ultimately the problem was solved by installing smoke washing machinery to remove the grit, and by fitting baffles in the funnels, which increased the velocity of ejection of the smoke and shot it straight up into the air. By the time it came down the ship had gone. This washing plant itself had teething troubles, and was prone in its early days to priming, when it would shoot great gouts of filthy black gritty water out of the funnels, and I remember one embarrassing occasion when one of these dollops scored a direct hit on an expensively dressed American lady.

After the *Queen Mary* had been in service for about a year, every engineer officer was asked to submit suggestions for improvements which might be incorporated in the new liner—the *Queen Elizabeth*—which was then being built. Most of us had something to say on this score, and we heard later that many of the ideas put forward were in fact built into the new ship. Personally I was disappointed never to see the *Queen Elizabeth*—she did not sail until after war broke out, by which time I had left the company.

One of the troubles that had been anticipated in the *Queen Mary*, but which never really materialized, was vibration. The engineers installing our air conditioning plant had come to us straight from the French liner *Normandie*, and told us horrific stories of the vibration in that ship. Apparently this was so bad that she had to slow down at meal times to enable the passengers to eat, and also at night so that they could sleep, and we were told that there were pantries on the ship where beer tankards would not stay on the cup hooks screwed into the deckhead.

The *Queen Mary* certainly did have some vibration in the after part of the ship in bad weather, when the screws carrying up to 200,000 hp would tend to lift out of the water, but generally speaking she gave you a smooth ride, and when she was not rolling—a trouble I will deal with in the chapter on bad weather—it was often difficult to believe that you were at sea. Even in the after part of the ship the vibration was considerably less than in modern Isle of Wight ferries.

Many of the teething troubles experienced were dealt with satisfactorily while at sea, but

there were some that could only be tackled in port when the ship was practically shut down. As we were only in Southampton from Monday night to Wednesday morning this sometimes meant non-stop work for the engineers, and there were occasions when some of us never got off the ship during the turn round. In fact I remember one period of gales which coincided with a lot of maintenance work when I did not see daylight for a month. At times like these we remembered the Superintendent's words about having to put the ship first.

On one eastward trip there was an accident to the high pressure turbine of one of the engines, and a number of blades were stripped out. As previously mentioned there was actually a total

Left *Leaving Pier 90 on an eastbound voyage.*

Below *A few of the many massive and powerful ovens in the galleys. When the cooks came on duty at 6.00 am their first thought was to switch everything on, and on the Hotel Services Switchboard we had to watch out for the sudden increase in load* (University Archives, University of Liverpool).

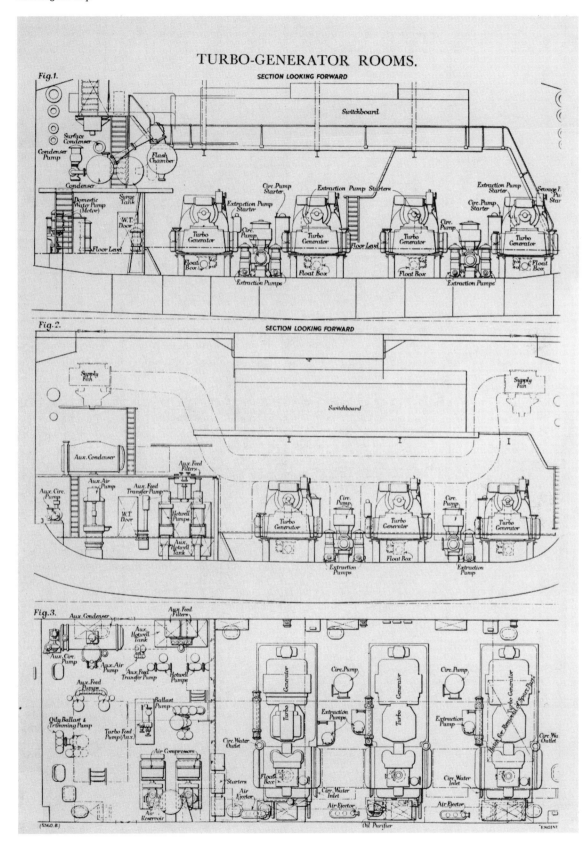

TURBO-GENERATOR ROOMS.

Above *In the graving dock for her annual overhaul, Christmas 1937. The docking charges alone for this six weeks period exceeded £21,000. Note her draft, marked on the stern in good old-fashioned English feet* (University Archives, University of Liverpool).

Left *In the King George V graving dock, Southampton. Compare the size of the bow with the men on the dock floor* (University Archives, University of Liverpool).

of 257,000 blades in the main propulsion turbines, all of them fitted by hand. The damaged
engine was shut down on reaching Cherbourg,
and as we crossed the Channel the lagging on the
high pressure cylinder was removed so that it
could cool down. By the time we reached
Southampton the cover was off and the rotor
ready for going ashore. The dockside crane that
was to pick it up lowered its hook through the
engine room skylight before the ship had come to
rest and the damaged rotor was on a lorry and off
to Thorneycrofts for repair before the ship was
moored up. A very smart piece of work indeed.
The rotor was re-bladed and was back in the ship
before we sailed on Wednesday.

I wish it were possible to be as complimentary
about the Thorneycroft night shift maintenance
gang that came aboard to work in Southampton,
but they were a lazy lot. As soon as the ship was
quiet they would creep up on top of the boilers
where it was warm, and kip down for the night.
This used to infuriate those of us who were on
watch, and who perhaps had had a tiring trip
from New York, and we used to make it our
business to walk across the top of the boilers,
over their recumbent bodies, as often as possible.

Apart from the disgustingly lazy shore gang
the quick turnround of the ship was good to see.
The minute the ship came to rest conveyors were
pushed up from the dock through shipside doors
and the changeover of dirty to clean linen, and

the re-victualling of the ship began. When you
consider that linen and provisions for 3,500
people for two weeks had to be loaded, you can
see what a mammoth task it was, and that the
organization necessary to perform it quickly and
efficiently must have been of a high order. Normally the operation had to be carried out in about
36 hours, but when we were late back and there
was little time I have seen it completed in less
than twelve hours.

Once a year the *Queen Mary* was put into the
King George V Dry Dock in Southampton to
have her bottom attended to and to have her
propellers changed if necessary. It was quite an
experience to walk about underneath this giant,
and rather shattering that one could hear so
much of what was going on inside. It was

Right *Machinery Supply Switchboard, controlling four
generators that supplied power for the auxiliaries used in
connection with the propulsion of the ship. The telegraph
is the slave to the one mounted in the Forward Engine
Room* (University Archives, University of Liverpool).

Below right *Plan of* Queen Mary's *main kitchens.*

Below *Rudder and starboard side propellers. The
rudder was hollow and fitted with a door. Inside was a
permanent iron ladder for inspection purposes* (University Archives, University of Liverpool).

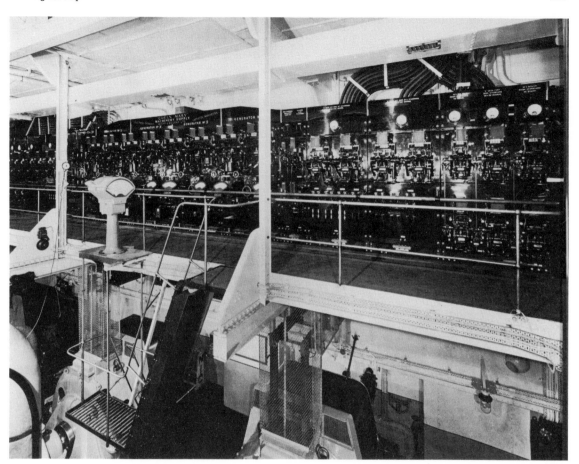

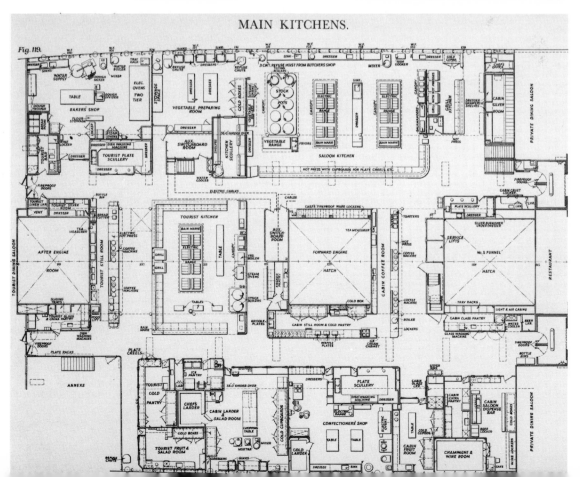

MAIN KITCHENS.

The Navigating Bridge, where the ultimate decisions had to be taken. The four symmetrically placed telegraphs each controlled one of the main engines (University Archives, University of Liverpool).

possible to recognize the voices of engineers in the generating stations, and it was rather a solemn thought that at sea there was only a ¾ in steel plate between you and the ocean.

On one occasion when we were in dry dock the City of Southampton held a black-out drill in the town and we were asked to blacken the *Queen Mary*. As luck would have it I was the duty electrician, and when I started to black out the ship I soon realized that so many odd lights had been left on in the cabins that the only way to do the job was to black out the whole of the passenger accommodation from the various sub-stations. I carried a torch with me so that I could see where I was going, but did not realize that the engineer on watch on the turbo-generator had nipped up to his cabin for a few minutes. He was on his way back to the engine room when all the lights went out, and there is nothing so dark as the inside of a ship. We were not amused.

Actually there was often a bit of 'needle' between the steam engineers and the electricians. After all, this was the first ship in which all the auxiliaries were driven by electricity, and the steam engineers rather resented this and were suspicious of what we did. Perhaps they felt they were rather in our power. I once heard an unbelievable but illuminating argument between Roberts, the Chief Engineer, and Hann, the Chief Electrician, about the power carried by electric cables. The former could not comprehend how a wire no thicker than your little finger could transmit more power than a steam pipe 18 in in diameter. His bewilderment was shared by the majority of his 63 underlings, so that it was comparatively easy to pull their legs.

Some of the steam engineers were incredibly ham-fisted, and were accustomed to using brute force in turning large steam valves by means of a wheel-key. They seemed quite at a loss when faced with comparatively small and light electrical switchgear, and their treatment of this type of equipment made one wince. One of the instruments provided for their use in the boiler rooms was a salinometer, which tested the

Close up of an engine telegraph. Every movement of the handles was repeated on a similar telegraph in the engine room, to the accompaniment of a clanging bell (University Archives, University of Liverpool).

John Rennie, resplendent in 'Whites'.

amount of salt in the boiler feed water. This instrument was based on a Wheatstone Bridge and had small knobs on the rheostats which altered the electrical resistance of the circuits. These knobs were frequently twisted right off by the engineer operating the instrument, and one wondered how he got on at home with his wireless set.

The other people who did not understand about electricity were the cooks in the kitchen. They came on duty at 6.00 am and their first thought was to walk round the galleys switching on every piece of electrical equipment they had. Down below on the switchboard it was uncanny to see the load steadily rising, and it was necessary to have another generator ready to cope with this—which amounted to an extra 1,000 amps of load within about ten minutes. A similar increase in load used to occur when leaving port. Once the signal 'Full Speed Ahead' had been received from the bridge all the pumps, fans, etc, and other auxiliaries were speeded up at the same time, and unless you were ready with a spare generator you could be in trouble.

A somewhat similar situation of fluctuating load sometimes occurred in mid-Atlantic when travelling along the edge of, and parallel to, the Gulf Stream whose waters were 10 degrees warmer than the surrounding ocean. Along the edge of the Stream we were continually running in and out of patches of warm water, and the speed of the condensing pumps was frequently being altered to suit, causing the electrical load to jump up and down.

Up on the bridge the deck officers had their own problems, though these were of a slightly different nature. They were all skilled and qualified navigators of course, but one morning I was up on the bridge and wandered into the Chart Room. The junior Officer of the Watch was making up the log and fiddling with a chart and a pair of dividers, so to make conversation I asked him where we were. 'Blowed if I know,' he said. 'What with the course Liverpool said we were to take, the course we are actually on, and the one that goes down in the book, it is very difficult to say!'

Actually their navigation was always very good, and they never missed America, but sometimes to the outsider it looked a little casual, and was what I used to call 'navigation by echo sounder'. From Newfoundland there is a long tapering ledge of rock sticking out under the sea to the south, and as you approach the American coast you must cross over this. On either side of this ledge the water is very deep, but very much more shallow on the ledge. One of the deck officers showed me how, when approaching the ledge they switched on their recording echo sounder which drew a continuous trace on a chart. As the ship passed from the deep water to the shallow, the needle of the recorder would jump a couple of inches indicating the change in depth, and when the ship passed into the deep water again the needle would move back. From the trace on the recorder chart it was possible to measure the width of this tapered ledge where the ship had crossed it, and hence by reference to the chart of the ocean they could say exactly where the ship was. It may sound a bit happy-go-lucky, but it seemed to work.

On 1 May an order would come down from the bridge that white cap covers would be worn, and from this we took it that summer had officially arrived. If and when we got a really hot summery day another order would reach us that the rig of the day would be 'Whites', and we would accordingly have to change our uniforms. Our white uniforms, when clean, were very smart—the jacket buttoned up to the neck, and badges of rank worn as epaulettes on the shoulder. They did not stay clean very long, and frequently had to be sent to the laundry, but they were cooler to wear than the thick blue reefer jackets of the normal uniform. On hot days, when we were sailing across a calm, deep ultramarine blue sea without a cloud in the sky, life on this great ship could be very pleasant.

Chapter 10

Life afloat

If it is true to say (and of course it is) that life is all about people, then it follows that there is abundant life in an Atlantic liner, for a liner houses more people per cubic foot than any other type of building. A ship such as the *Queen Mary* was after all a metal box in which a large number of people of all shapes and sizes, religions, creeds, and shades of political thought, were herded together and pushed out into a hostile and uncomfortable element to fend for themselves for five days. During this time they had to rely entirely on their own resources, only a very small number of them being able to maintain any contact at all with the outside world.

To the average passenger on a voyage of such short duration his appreciation of this unique situation is probably clouded by excitement, novelty, strange food, seasickness and apprehension, but the crew who live permanently in this environment react in a very different way. There is something rather odd about a ship, quite apart from its size and shape and the function it performs, a peculiar character which in some way pervades the whole existence of the crew, and subconsciously influences and changes their attitude to life.

Maybe this oddness is a very simple thing, based on the fact that the ship is not only your workplace, and your home, but also your security. In fact, it is your very life. Ashore, if you do not like the building you work in, or live in, you may leave it, at any time, day or night, at will. At sea you have no such choice. The ship restrains you, controls you, mothers you. She may upset you, but she gives you that priceless commodity —life—and never lets you forget it.

Is this why a ship is invariably referred to as 'she'? It is of course men who have invested ships with femininity, and apart from the way in which a ship will care for, and mother, her crew, there is a strong resemblance between a ship and a woman in the capricious way she behaves.

Every ship has her own individual way of behaving in a seaway. Some ride the waves serenely with the dignity of a dowager, while others frisk about in an almost wanton fashion; some will wallow, others will plunge their heads into an oncoming wave as if trying to commit suicide. But all, without exception, are feminine.

The *Queen Mary* was exceptionally good in a head sea, though occasionally she would put her nose into quite a moderate sized wave with a crash that shook the very teeth in your head. I watched her do this one day in a bit of a blow, and each time a slightly larger one came along she crashed into it as though it was the end of the world. Then an extra big brute turned up and you braced yourself for the shock—but this never came, she just brushed it aside as though it did not exist. She then put her nose down into a comparatively small one—just to show you.

This illogicality is a very feminine trait, and is guaranteed to keep a man interested, whether it is displayed by a ship or a woman. In fact, most men are suckers for this type of capricious behaviour and respond to it by producing a dog-like devotion which is remarkable to behold. I suppose the explanation is that every man has a need to love and be loved, a need to work for someone rather than himself, a need for something or someone of which to be proud. Not every man is lucky enough to find his ideal woman, but many many men find a satisfactory sublimation of this need by going to sea.

When I first joined the *Queen Mary* I was

surprised to find so many men, of such differing types, all working together more or less harmoniously, yet all grumbling about something or other. They grumbled persistently about the weather, the Skipper, the food, the government, or because Liverpool had been beaten by Manchester United, but most of all their grumbles were about their life at sea, and how much better off they would be ashore. When I taxed one or two of them about this and asked why they did not give up the sea and take a shore job, I was puzzled by the invariable response of blank amazement that anyone should even suggest such an unthinkable thing.

When I had been at sea a little longer I found out the reason why men stay at sea in spite of the hardships, the long hours (our normal weekly hours could vary between 56 and about 92) and the days and weeks spent away from home. The reason was a very simple one, and though I stumbled upon it by accident, and did not believe it at first, and have never been able to explain it, it is nevertheless true.

One winter's day, when the ship was due to sail I caught my tram as usual to go down to the docks. It was dark, cold, pouring with rain, and I was miserable. I had recently been married and we were very comfortable in our flat in the Polygon. I did not want to leave my warm and cosy home to be tossed about on that wretched Atlantic. We were short of money, and I had put off paying the electricity bill to the point that I was now worried that they might come and turn it off. My shoes needed repairing and I had stepped into a puddle with the one that was leaking. The tram was full of silent, wet, rather objectionable bodies, and jolted to and fro in a disgusting way.

In short, I was full of all the normal petty irritations and worries which are associated with life on the land. Two days later we were well out into the Atlantic, heading into a moderately rough sea, but I was on deck, leaning on the rail, smoking my pipe, and gazing at the water. I tried to remember all the troubles that had beset me when I left home, and though I could remember what they were, I was completely unable to stir up any emotion about any of them. They had all retreated into the background, and had no more substance or reality than last night's bad dream. I was shocked to find that I did not have a care in the world. My pipe was drawing evenly, the sea stretched away to the horizon on all sides, and I was at peace.

This then was the secret. On land, life becomes complicated, and the rhythm of life is a short,

Author, off watch.

sharp, staccato one. But at sea everything is simplified and reduced to basic principles and the values by which one lives are the true values. Your whole life is bound up in the life of the ship, nothing else matters, and the further you get away from England the less real your land life appears to be. You have in fact exchanged a staccato for a legato rhythm, a nightmare for a spell of blissful sleep, and there is little wonder that men find this so attractive. In the *Queen Mary* one senior engineer was the third generation of his family that had served the Cunard Company. Another had lost his father in the *Titanic*. Also there is something restful and soothing about sweetly running machinery, and providing you were prepared to work hard when the necessity arose the normal day's routine was calm and unhurried, with little to do.

In reasonable weather life for the engineer officers aboard the *Queen Mary* could be very pleasant. Our accommodation was comfortably furnished, and the standard of living good. When the ship first went into service the engineers' accommodation was in two sections. The seniors had very superior outside single cabins on the top deck aft near the Verandah Grill, but the juniors occupied a big block of cabins on E-Deck, most of them with no natural light or ventilation, and approached by a single companion way from the Working Alleyway. Some of these cabins were a bit noisy, particularly in the early morning when the stewards were wheeling stores about overhead, and one cabin at least was next to a cold store and had a bulkhead perpetually covered in frost.

But the biggest disadvantage of this block of accommodation was its single entrance, and it was felt that in the event of a fire many engineers would be trapped, with unpleasant consequences. Several engineers took this up with the Navigating and Engineer Officers' Union, with swift and satisfactory results, for in our first lay-up a new block of accommodation was built on top of the Verandah Grill, and we were all then very much closer to the fresh air, and to our Ward Room which was on the deck below. The price we paid for this improvement was that some of the junior juniors had to double up, and give up the luxury of a single cabin.

The Union was naturally jubilant at this success, for which they took all the credit, and every engineer officer was asked to join. This was my first real experience of Union activity, but not having heard the company side of the argument, and not wishing to appear a rebel at this early stage in my sea-going career, I refrained from joining, but must confess to having always felt slightly guilty about this.

Our mess room on D-Deck was supplied from the Cabin Class Galley, and the food was really extremely good. We had the Cabin Class menu, and in theory we could order any dish off this extensive card. Over a period one naturally experimented with different dishes, but gradually settled down to a varied but reasonable diet, about which nobody could really complain.

A glance at a typical menu will show the scale of the cuisine which was offered to Cabin Class passengers. The menu itself was printed on a double card the outside of which contained a reproduction of one or other of the many art treasures in the ship. Luncheon and dinner menus each day were quite different, were individually dated, and each contained about eighty dishes. The breakfast menu was simpler, being a single sheet, but it actually listed over a hundred different items, and after all these years I can still remember the shirred eggs and grilled York ham which was a favourite breakfast dish of mine, particularly when on the 4 to 8 watch. There is no accounting for tastes however, and one American passenger confided in me that his favourite breakfast was the meat off a kipper, beaten up in a glass of milk with strawberry jam. This dish was *not* listed on the menu!

In the service pantry next to the mess room was a water boiler, a pop-up toaster and a fridge, so that when going on watch in the early hours it was always possible to make yourself a snack. The fridge contained butter, milk, and jams, etc, and large tins of fruit juice—orange, pineapple, grapefruit, and prune. The latter was particularly refreshing when coming off watch after four hours in the heat of the engine rooms. When the ship was in the Gulf Stream in the summer the humidity was very high—though not as unbearable as in New York City—and down below the temperature could reach 105 degrees Fahrenheit. Under these conditions one wore only a boiler suit and could feel the perspiration trickling down one's body, so that copious draughts of liquids were very necessary. Tea and coffee were always available if a hot drink was required, and altogether we were pretty well catered for. There was one occasion when the tea began to taste a bit, and on investigation we found a dead rat in the water boiler, but apart from this we had no trouble.

A breakfast menu, Cabin Class.

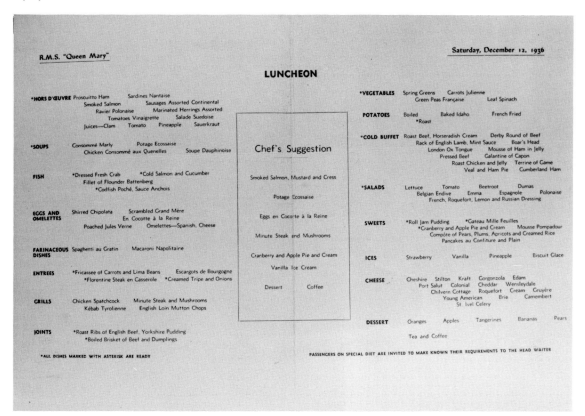

Above *Typical Cabin Class luncheon menus.*
Below *Verandah Grill luncheon menu.*

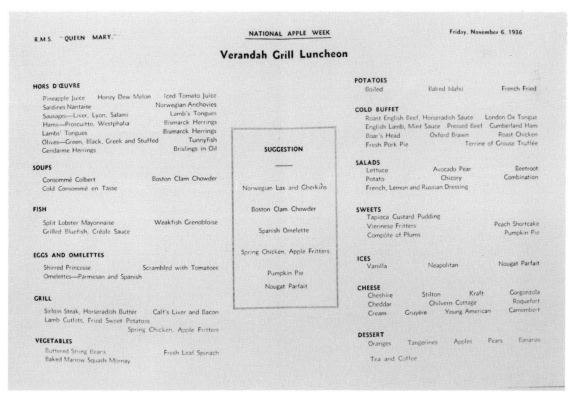

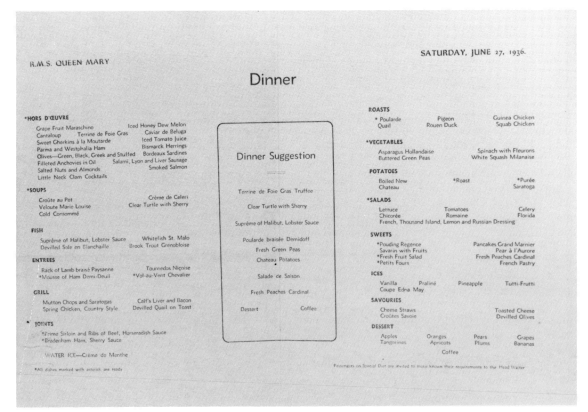

Above *Typical dinner menu, Cabin Class.*
Below *Independence Day dinner menu, Cabin Class.*

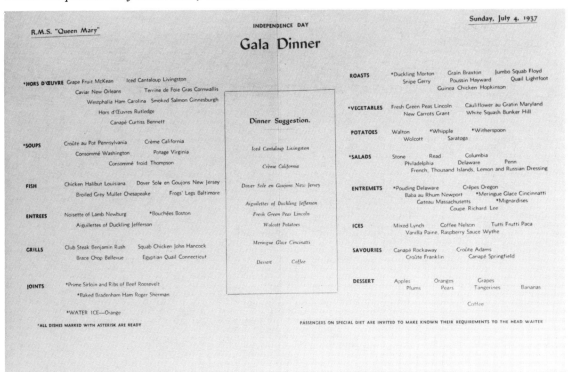

The engineers' wardroom was very well appointed and comfortable. It was situated on the port side of the Sun Deck, forward of the Verandah Grill, and had large windows which made it very light and airy. It had its own library containing several hundred books, a full sized table tennis table, and several card tables. Table tennis and cribbage were our favourite games, the former being especially popular. We ran a table tennis 'ladder', which listed players according to skill, and by challenging the man ahead of you, and beating him, you changed places with him on the ladder. The man at the top was designated Champion of the North Atlantic, and I once occupied this dizzy pinnacle for a short time.

Playing table tennis when the ship was rolling badly introduced a new and interesting element into the game. With care and practice, and a certain amount of luck, it was possible to use the roll to baffle your opponent, some shots which on an even keel would have been off the table just managing to clip the edge when the ship was rolling the right way.

The cabin I shared with another engineer was very comfortable and had only one snag. It was an inside cabin situated immediately above the forward end of the Verandah Grill, and part of the ship's main mast went up through the wardrobe. The Verandah Grill was really the ship's night club and catered for late night revellers. It had a four-piece group consisting of piano, saxophone, drums and double bass, and they dispensed dance music until the early hours. It was not possible to hear the music in my cabin, but the double bass player stood alongside the main mast as it passed through the room, and this hollow metal tube acted as a sounding board. As I lay in my bunk, trying to sleep, all I could hear, emanating from the wardrobe, was oomp-pah, oomp-pah, oomp-pah . . . and there were many occasions when I wished this musician would in fact stick it up his jumper.

As mentioned in a previous chapter, sleep was a great problem in this ship, due mainly to the daily clock change, though there were other factors. The *Queen Mary* was fitted extensively with Dunlopillo mattresses, which were a comparatively new feature in those days, and several engineers complained bitterly that though comfortable these mattresses 'drew the body' and were too hot. Sleep had to be taken in two separate spells anyway, except for those lucky enough to be on day work, and the ability to be able to go to sleep for an hour whenever the opportunity afforded was a habit to be much

'Farewell Dinner' menu, usually a Sunday evening affair.

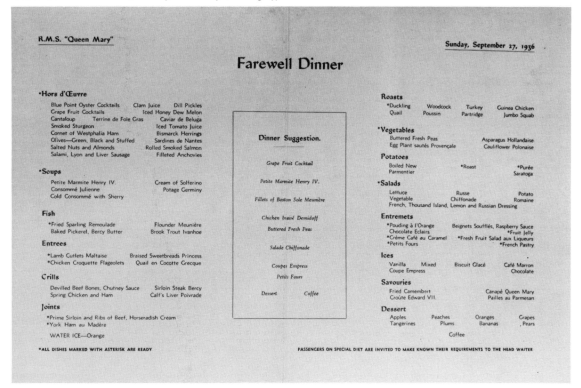

R.M.S. "QUEEN MARY"   Tuesday, September 29, 1936

Dinner

Cantaloup   Grape Fruit
Hors d'Œuvre Variés

Croute au Pot   Green Pea Soup Longchamps

Halibut Hollandaise
Fried Fillets of Sole Tartare

Tournedos sautés Ambassadeur

TO ORDER FROM THE GRILL:
Lamb Chops Saratogas   Spring Chicken and Bacon

Roast Beef, Horseradish Sauce
Baked Ham, Sherry Sauce
Roast Chicken à l'Anglaise

Cauliflower, Cream Sauce   French Beans sautés
Boiled, Chateau and Purée Potatoes

Salade de Saison

Pouding Soufflé aux Fruits   Cream Caramel
Peaches Melba   Pastry   Petits Fours
Vanilla, Nesselrode and Strawberry Ices

Dessert   Coffee

Above *Third Class dinner menu.*

Above right *Special cover for Independence Day dinner menu.*

prized. On top of all the factors—watch keeping, clock changing, bad weather, etc,—striving to keep you awake except when you were on watch, there was another one which used to attack the crew on the Sunday night before we reached England.

This was called Channel fever and seemed to strike all and sundry without discrimination. It was a strange complaint, its only symptom being an inability to sleep the night before you were due home, and I suppose it was something akin to the contagion that children pick up on Christmas Eve. It struck with unfailing regularity and many engineers accepted it as inevitable and sat up all night either playing cards or reading.

In the summer, and depending on which watch you were on, there were plenty of opportunities for sun-bathing. The engineers had their own piece of deck, and it was extremely pleasant to lie out in the sun when the ship was just rolling lazily to the swell, and soak up the sunshine. It was also very dangerous to do this in mid-Atlantic, for the sun's rays were deceptively hot, and it was very easy to get burned. Jackie Brinton, my room-mate, once had the misfortune to fall asleep for about an hour while sunbathing, and the skin subsequently peeled off his back like stripping wallpaper.

At times the weather in the North Atlantic was almost tropical, and in calm spells we often sighted whales. We also saw flying fish on occasion, and I once saw an enormous turtle. No one would believe me about this, but nevertheless it was true. I happened to be looking over the side one afternoon and this huge creature was swimming away from the ship for all it was worth.

Each voyage one enterprising steward ran a sweepstake among the crew based on the football results, at 6d a ticket. The first prize was £10, which seemed a lot of money at the time, and twice when going on leave I was lucky enough to win it. To an impecunious engineer this was extremely useful.

Leave was normally unheard of in British ships, and was a special feature introduced into the *Queen Mary* because of her peculiar problems of quick turn-round. Even when it was your turn to have a trip off, there was an element of uncertainty about it, as it was subject to your replacement turning up, and there being no absentees due to sickness or any other cause. On the Wednesday morning when your leave was due to start you had to report aboard the ship as usual, and it was not until the ship was due to sail that you were released and allowed to go ashore.

This was all very well if you had no commitments, but one trip when I was due to have leave I had arranged to get married, and there was no way in which I could be sure of being available until the ship had actually sailed. My fiancée was at home in Norfolk, where the wedding was to take place, and on Wednesday morning was waiting for a telephone call from me either to say that everything was OK, or that I was on my way to New York. Getting married under these conditions was therefore rather a chancy

business, but in the event we were lucky, and nothing occurred to prevent me getting to the church on time.

And so the weekly routine went on, backwards and forwards, backwards and forwards, until it felt sometimes rather like a bus service. Each Monday we would be arriving either in New York or in Cherbourg, the only variation coming once in a while when for some reason we also called at Plymouth. Little things broke the monotony, such as one Sunday evening a few hundred miles off Land's End when we passed a fully rigged sailing ship silhouetted against the sunset—an unforgettable sight. Then it was on to Cherbourg, and across the Channel to the Isle of Wight, up Spithead, round the Brambles Buoy and up Southampton Water. As we turned into the Ocean Dock there was one long blast on the whistle— known universally as the lodger's warning—and we were home.

The Verandah Grill. Note the section of the main mast that passed through the room. This was where the double bass player stood (University Archives, University of Liverpool).

Chapter 11

Life ashore

Until I joined the Cunard Company I had never been to Southampton, and my first feeling was one of delight. Here was a clean, fresh-faced town and seaport, bustling with activity, its docks full of shipping, trading with all parts of the world, a town showing every sign of prosperity and commercial enterprise. Previously my only experience of great seaports had been with Glasgow and Liverpool, both giving the impression of being rather dark, gloomy and forbidding places.

Southampton however was entirely different, being lighter, cleaner and having definitely a smiling countenance. Its modern civic centre—whose buildings reminded me irresistibly of Nottingham University, and must surely have been designed by the same archiect—was surrounded by gardens which were neat and tidy and full of flowers, and presented an image of 20th century efficiency. Yet many old houses, the town walls, the Bargate, and the waterfront, reminded one that the town was steeped in history and had been an important seaport for centuries.

The Romans established a settlement here in the first century AD but the present town is believed to be Anglo-Saxon in origin. Canute, the first Danish King of England, for some time made the place his residence, and there is a spot on the shore near the mouth of the River Itchen, traditionally known as Canute's Point, where this monarch is said to have rebuked his courtiers for their sycophancy in declaring that even the waves of the sea would obey his voice. By the time of Domesday in 1086 the town had given its name to the county of Southampton, and for several centuries the port was the most important one on the South Coast.

In the 14th century the town was visited several times by the marauding French, and it suffered dreadful losses from the plague known as the Black Death, which swept the country in 1348. Its fortunes revived however, and in August 1415 Henry V set sail from the port with his army to invade France, an expedition that culminated in the battle of Agincourt in October of the same year.

After a further period of decline as a commercial port, and a short spell in the 18th century as a fashionable seaside spa, Southampton's fortunes again began to look up in the early years of the 19th century with the invention of the steamship. Beginning with the setting up of ferry services to the Isle of Wight and the Channel Islands, and followed soon after by the establishment of a railway service between Southampton and London, and the building of the Eastern Docks, the port entered upon a period of growth and prosperity that was to last for a hundred years.

As ocean-going ships increased in size the docks were improved and expanded, and Southampton became successively the headquarters of the P&O Steam Navigation Company for their service to Spain, Portugal, the Mediterranean, and India; the Royal Mail Steam Packet Company for their West Indian and American service; the North German Lloyd Company; the Hamburg-America Line; and in 1856 the Union Line which eventually amalgamated with the Castle Line.

In 1911 the White Star Line introduced the first of three new luxury liners, the *Olympic*, and the Ocean Dock, which was later to become the home of the *Queen Mary*, was built specifically for these three ships. (The second was the

Titanic, which hit an iceberg on her maiden voyage and sank, and the third, the *Gigantic*, after the *Titanic* disaster, was discreetly re-named the *Britannic*.)

In 1919 the Cunard Company made Southampton the English end of their transatlantic service to New York, and fifteen years later, in 1934—the year the *Queen Mary* was launched—the merger between Cunard and White Star took place, a merger that virtually saw the end of the White Star Company.

When the *Queen Mary* arrived and made Southampton her home port, John Rennie and I had to find somewhere to live, all the other engineers already having homes in the town. With the help of the company we found digs with a Miss Miller in a nice house in the Polygon district, only a short tram ride from the docks. Miss Miller was a lady of ample proportions, with a heart of gold of commensurate size, and she made us very welcome. She was a good cook and looked after us well in spite of our strange and rather unusual working hours.

We would leave for work at 4.30 in the after-noon and return home for breakfast at 8.30 the following morning. In theory we had both been up all night, but in practice it was possible to get a little sleep—there was literally nothing to do if the one generator continued to run peacefully, and in all the time I was in the ship the BTH generators gave no trouble at all—so that when the weather was fine we were raring to be out, exploring the neighbourhood.

We found a small garage in Shirley that had a car for hire, and this widened our horizons to include the New Forest, a district that neither of us knew. In this way I made acquaintance with many famous beauty spots, and particularly with Beaulieu and Bucklers Hard, both of which were to become very familiar places to me when later on I became an amateur sailor and kept my boat on a mooring in the Beaulieu River.

The other discovery we made, which in my case turned into a life-long friendship, was to find the Isle of Wight. Red Funnel Steamers ran a passenger service of small ships from Southampton to Cowes, and it was possible to catch a boat in the early morning, have breakfast on board, and be in Cowes by about 9.30 am. I found the island very different from the main-land, and wholly delightful, and though we were not able to spend very much time exploring, we found out enough to send me back time and time again. The island has never ceased to fascinate me, and it would take several lifetimes to explore it thoroughly and savour all its delights.

When, later in 1936, I got married, it was natural that our first home in Southampton should be a flat in Morris Road, The Polygon, only just around the corner from Miss Miller's house. The engineer officers subscribed to buy us a chiming grandmother clock as a wedding present, and this was formally presented to me in mid-Atlantic by the Chief Engineer. The clock, minus its pendulum and chimes, spent a hazar-dous voyage wedged in my wardrobe, and I was very relieved once it safely reached home.

Memories of those early years of married life in Southampton are a bit mixed as I was home only once a fortnight and then only for a few hours. Over Christmas the ship went into dry dock and most engineers were able to spend a few days at home, but the switchboard had to be manned, and I can well remember the cloud of gloom in which I rode my bicycle down to the dry dock on Christmas Day.

One of the happy memories concerns the little church of St Julian in the old part of the town which my wife used to attend when I was away. This church was given to French Huguenot refugees in the 17th century for their exclusive use, and the services there, though the standard Church of England services, were still con-ducted in French. On the one occasion when I was home on a Sunday I attended Evensong at this church. A prayer for those at sea was always included in the service, and I found the know-ledge of this a very real comfort, particularly in storms, which frequently seemed to blow up on a Sunday.

At this time Southampton was a very pleasant place in which to live, and was a typical medium sized English town. The sounds of ships were always there to remind you that it was an important seaport. The city at the other end of our Atlantic crossing, New York, could not have been a greater contrast. Both in character, and in the tempo of its life, it was the antithesis of everything English, being noisy, dirty, cosmopolitan, and brash. Amongst the impressions recalled earlier (Chapter 7) I was struck by the fact that at 9.30 pm the next day's morning papers appeared on the streets, papers huge in size and containing several sections, many of them printed in English, Yiddish, Italian, and German. By midnight the pavements were littered with papers that had simply been discarded by their owners, along with other types of refuse. Broadway, Times Square, and several other main streets were lit up by a multiplicity of neon signs, the traffic was intense and noisy, there was much raucous

St Julian's Church in Winkle Street, Southampton, where services to this day are conducted in French (Southampton City Archives).

music, and many strange smells.

But let it not be thought that New York was just a kind of Soho on a larger and more distorted scale. It was obviously much more than that, and indeed a very wonderful city, but inevitably the view of a visiting sailor was coloured by the rather sleazy streets between Pier 90 on 50th Street and Times Square and further downtown. Many of the more elegant and fashionable parts of the city I never got to see.

There were plenty of places of interest, however, that I was able to visit, such as the Planetarium, something quite new to me and very fascinating, and the Metropolitan Museum which was on a par with our own South Kensington. Their Egyptian rooms were incredible, stocked with so many treasures that one was forced to the conclusion that the Americans had stolen more from Egypt than the English— which some may find difficult to believe.

Other places I was grateful to have the opportunity to visit included Central Park, the Bowery, The Bronx Zoo, Wall Street, Coney Island, and Palisades Park. But it was perhaps to be expected that it was the theatres, concert halls, and other places of entertainment that provided the greatest variety, each in its own way producing a high standard, and one that was never likely to be met in Southampton. For instance, I was able to attend a Toscanini concert, which was quite an experience, several serious plays, song and dance shows at Radio City Music Hall—where they had a chorus of over 100 lissom and high kicking ladies—ice hockey at Madison Square Garden, and various revues and musical comedies for which free tickets were sent to the ship. One such revue was called 'New Faces of 1936' with music by Cole Porter. The show itself was mediocre and did not survive for very long, but the music lived on and turned up in another show in England some years later.

The theatre in New York at this time presented a curious mixture of entertainments, from opera and ballet down to a fairly basic strip-tease, with practically every other type of entertainment in between: in fact the whole gamut from Minsky to Nijinsky—Minsky's Burlesque Theatre on Broadway being the most celebrated strip-tease joint in town.

Minsky's was quite literally an eye-opener. It was the first 'permissive' theatre I had ever visited, where the chorus was topless and, to my youthful eye, middle-aged, and where the sketches were all smutty and not very funny. It was my first experience of seeing men climbing over the seats to get to the front. One of the principal attractions was a girl called Gypsy Rose Lee, who later became a legendary figure.

The musical comedy stage was also more permissive than in England, and one show I remember was called 'Red, Hot, and Blue'. This was a slick and efficient production the theme of which was the search for a girl of 21 who had just inherited a million dollars. When she was a little girl she had been kidnapped, and nobody knew what had become of her. The only clue to her identity was that just before the kidnapping she had had the misfortune to sit on a hot waffle iron, the scars of which she was still believed to bear, so that every claimaint—and there were several—had to be inspected, and this was carried out down stage centre.

The three stars in this show were an interesting bunch, the leading lady being Ethel Merman, who was then at the height of her powers. Her part was that of a rich but sexually frustrated woman who lived in an expensive penthouse. Her principal number was a torch song entitled *Down in the Dumps on the 90th Floor*, which contained the classic couplet 'Even the Janitor's wife has a perfectly good love life'.

The comedian was Schnozzle Durante, who contributed quite considerably to the success of the show, and the juvenile lead, believe it or not,

was a rather plump and flabby young man called Bob Hope, who oozed about the stage, and whose most memorable line—repeated ad nauseam—was 'Oh my Gard!' I believe that at this time he had not yet broken into films, and changed his image, but in this particular show he did not strike me as a very pleasant character.

Another performer I saw on the stage was Mae West. She was very popular at the time and was filling a theatre on Broadway with her own brand of humour. Her show opened with a situation which has since become part of the Mae West legend, and which demonstrated her appreciation of the need to open a show with a bang, and get a quick laugh.

When the curtain went up she was lying on a chaise longue in a very seductive attitude, and her negress maid—an enormous woman—came in and said 'Oh Miss West, there are nine guys downstairs waiting to see you.' To which Mae replied 'Oh,' (and no one but Mae West has ever got such a wealth of meaning into that simple little word) 'Oh, I'm tired. One of those guys will have to wait.' The shout of laughter that greeted this sally told her that once again she had an audience safely in her pocket. After this she could do no wrong.

The concert I remember most vividly was one given by Benny Goodman and his Orchestra, for this concert was the first occasion on which an audience was 'sent'. It has since become quite commonplace for an audience, particularly of young people, to go wild and shout and scream, but it had to start somewhere, and it started here in the Coliseum Theatre in New York at this concert.

The Coliseum was claimed to be the largest theatre in the world, housing several thousands, and I remember that to get up to the back of the Circle it was necessary to take a lift. On this particular occasion the theatre was full, and the concert started quietly enough. The band line-up was impressive, and after a few numbers by the whole orchestra, the Benny Goodman Quartet took over for a spell. This featured Gene Krupa on drums, Teddy Wilson on piano, Lionel Hampton on Vibraphone, and of course Benny Goodman on clarinet.

I think it was the Quartet that started the excitement, although it was the big band that really roused the audience to frenzy. Towards the end of the concert people were fainting and being carried out in droves, and it was altogether an unforgettable experience. Subsequently there was much comment on how this audience reaction had come about, and I believe Goodman himself said it was done by pitching the beat in time to the natural heart beat, and then gradually quickening it. My main recollection of the evening is of the girl—a complete stranger—sitting next to me who lost many of her inhibitions and kept clutching me. Music has strange powers!

The shops also in New York were strange to English eyes. Supermarkets, I suppose, were a natural development from departmental stores and the 5 and 10 cent stores like Woolworths, and America was way ahead of us in this—as in many other things. (I once had an argument with a boastful American who claimed that his country was years ahead of ours in every way—until I pointed out that however far ahead they might think they are, in point of fact they are always, perpetually, five hours behind.)

One of the most fascinating shops of the supermarket type was Maceys, a huge block of a building down town which sold practically everything, and in which it was possible to spend hours just wandering round marvelling at the merchandise and the way it was displayed. On one of our trips, in their furniture department, they were staging a campaign to sell 'English' furniture, and this brought home to one the almost unbelievable fascination most Americans had for anything English. The centre piece of this sales campaign was a series of about six rooms furnished in what was described as typically English styles. These rooms were quite extraordinary, and no more English in character than a Chinese temple, the walls being covered with the busiest and vilest types of Victorian wallpaper, and the rooms crammed with the kind of furniture one would only expect to find in a jumble sale. But the area was thronged with people, and good business was being done.

Another intriguing type of shop was the Automat, a completely automated restaurant serving a wide variety of hot and cold food. There were several of these Automats about the city, all equally efficient and popular. Each dish was contained in a glass-fronted, coin-operated locker, the banks of lockers being in effect the wall of the kitchen, from which they were fed from behind. As you went in at the door there was a young man sitting at a desk dispensing change, the only coins needed in the restaurant being dimes, and in many ways this giving of change was the most fascinating feature of the restaurant. He had a huge stack of dimes and could whip off ten to the dollar with the speed of light and without counting. If you checked to see if he had given you the right number he was quite

hurt.

One of the commodities I regularly bought in New York was tobacco, for in those days I was a pipe smoker. In England good quality Virginia tobacco cost 9d an ounce, and there was one superlative brand—Edgeworth—that retailed at 2/6d for an ounce and a third. This was way beyond my normal pocket and I smoked it perhaps once a year, at Christmas time. But in America of course Virginia tobacco was cheap, and I was amazed and delighted to find Edgeworth costing only about 4d an ounce. So I got into the habit of buying a ½ lb tin each trip, and in Southampton—where duty had to be paid on tins of tobacco—transferred it into an airtight container a pouchful at a time.

My affection for New York varied with the seasons. In the spring and in the autumn there were some bright, sharp days of such a magic quality that you would not wish to be anywhere else, but the winter was hard and bitter, and the summer was so hot and humid as to be frightening. At times in the summer it felt as though you were breathing through a hot wet blanket, and this was most unpleasant. The only way to get cool was to lie in a cold bath, and even this only gave temporary relief, for the very effort of drying yourself and walking back to your cabin, made you just as hot again.

Going ashore in these conditions was not always pleasant, and you had to be very keen in order to make the effort. On 50th Street and the surrounding area were many blocks of brown-stone tenement buildings, all seemingly over-populated, and living in them must have been very unpleasant. As you walked to and from the ship you passed many such blocks, and an abiding recollection is of the inhabitants sitting outside on the steps in a vain attempt to keep cool.

The nights were just as oppressive as the days, and a few of us got together and devised a pleasant way of cooling off after we had been ashore in the evening. The Tourist swimming pool was way down in the bowels of the ship aft, and we made sure that this was filled with clean water just before we reached New York. Here we were out of the way of everyone, and were not doing any harm, and our midnight swimming parties are amongst my most pleasant recollections of New York.

In this sort of weather it was always a relief to leave America and head out east, where at least there was air to breathe, though when we got into the warm waters of the Gulf Stream it could again be pretty hot and sticky.

Chapter 12

Bad weather

In the winter of 1936-37 the weather in the North Atlantic was reputed to be the worst in living memory. I was in no way able to comment on this as it was the first time I had seen this particular ocean, but we certainly had our share of storms. The Atlantic is, however, an ocean of extreme moods, which can change very rapidly.

As has been said, the weather is greatly influenced by the Gulf Stream, the warm water current which rises in the Gulf of Mexico, travels north parallel to the American coast, and then crosses the Atlantic to Europe. This mass of warm water in mid-Atlantic, together with the ice which drifts down from the north, has a strange effect on the weather, the whole region being subject to violent storms. In addition, when the intensely cold water associated with the ice reaches the Gulf Stream the result can be a fairly extensive area of fog. The weather can, in consequence, fluctuate rapidly from flat calms to ferocious tempests, from blue skies and sunshine to dank, impenetrable fog. Even in the middle of winter I have seen the sea absolutely still, without a ripple on its surface, and in summer have seen the same sea whipped up by furious winds into large and menacing waves.

The size of waves is a subject on which many travellers tend to exaggeration, and what I am now about to say may cause this accusation to be levelled against me. In defence all I can say is that the memory of some of the storms we encountered is still vividly with me, and anyone who regularly travelled the North Atlantic in the winter of 1936 will, I am sure, endorse the statement that we met some phenomenal wave patterns.

The *Queen Mary* was a large ship, and when viewed from a deck which is normally 100 ft above water level it is difficult to assess the size of the waves, or the distance from crest to crest, though the tendency is to under-estimate rather than exaggerate them. But in one particular storm I have seen that ship, which was over 1,000 ft long, down in a trough of a wave, with water piled up at the bow and the stern seemingly as high as the deck on which I was with difficulty standing. If my eyes were not deceiving me then, the distance from crest to crest of that particular wave must have been 1,100-1,200 ft, and the height approximately 100 ft. The experts may proclaim that such a mammoth wave is impossible, to which I can only reply that I wish they had been with me at the time, for it was a sight I shall never forget. Nor shall I forget the view a few moments later, when we climbed over the crest of this particular monster, and looked down into the valley below, a valley into which we rapidly plunged.

The Beaufort Wind Scale classifies all winds from light airs (Force 1) to hurricanes (Force 12), and also describes the sea conditions associated with each force of wind. For example, it is at Force 7 (near gale) that the tops of waves begin to be blown off in streaks along the direction of the wind. As the wind increases, and waves become bigger, so this streaking effect becomes more marked, until at Force 11 (violent storm) the waves are described as exceptionally high, up to 52 ft, small and medium sized ships perhaps being lost to view for a time behind them. The sea is completely covered with long white patches of foam, the edges of the wave crests being blown into froth. At Force 12 (hurricane), which describes a wind velocity of over 64 knots (74 mph) the air is filled with foam and spray, and the sea is completely white with driving spray, visibility being seriously affected.

What Beaufort does not comment on is the noise associated with all this tumult, for this is deafening. Nor does he, to my mind, sufficiently emphasize the interference with visibility. When you get up to Force 11 and Force 12 winds the effect is exactly as in a thick fog, and this was something I had not expected.

The *Queen Mary* was built in three sections, with expansion joints in between. These joints gave her hull a certain amount of flexibility, and I was told that without it she would have broken her back when riding over large waves.

I never fully understood how these expansion joints worked, but in storms you could hear them creaking away, and up on the Sun Deck the rail was not continuous where the joint came out, the two halves of the teak capping being joined together with a brass sleeve. When the ship was pitching badly you could see the rail sliding in and out of this sleeve over a distance of several inches. When the ship went into dry dock a surveyor's level was set up on one of the 800 ft long passenger alleyways, and when she settled on the blocks it was very interesting to see that she had 'sagged' by about 4 in.

Seeing the *Queen Mary* tied up in the dock, dwarfing the dockside cranes and all the buildings in the neighbourhood, it was easy to think that no power on earth could make her pitch and roll. But when you were 1,000 miles from the nearest land, and it was blowing a gale, you took a different view, and wondered how on earth this toy could continue to float. In a head sea she was a fine ship. Any ship will pitch if the seas are big enough, but the *Queen Mary* rode them well. True, she occasionally put her nose down into one and spooned up a few tons of solid water over the bow—and sometimes right over the top of the bridge—but generally she lifted to them so that all that came aboard was spray.

But brother, could she roll! To be absolutely honest this was her besetting sin, and it caused her passengers and crew a lot of inconvenience, and her owners a considerable amount of money to overcome. I do not think there was ever any question of her safety, but there was equally no doubt that in her first year of service she was an extremely uncomfortable ship in which to travel when the sea was following or on the beam. On one trip, in mid-Atlantic, we passed the *Berengaria* outward bound to New York. The sea was roughish but there was the old '*Bere*', steaming serenely on an even keel, while we, the new ship and pride of the fleet, were rolling wildly from side to side. Many of us felt embarrassed and wished our Skipper had kept us out of sight.

The first storm in which it became apparent that all was not well was not a particularly severe one, but she rolled 14 degrees either side of the vertical. That may not seem a very big angle but, to get a better idea of what it implies lay up your dining table for a meal, and then tilt it 14 degrees, first one way and then the other.

When this storm had subsided, and we were sailing on a more or less even keel again, I was up on deck one evening with another engineer who had been at sea for many years, and we were discussing the rolling to which we had recently been subjected. He told me of an experience he had had some years before in the *Aquitania* on a Mediterranean cruise. Apparently they had sailed past Cape Otranto into the Adriatic to be met suddenly by a very strong wind which was funnelling down from the Alps. As this wind hit the *Aquitania* she heeled over to an angle of 22 degrees, and caused some consternation aboard. I can see him now as he leaned on the rail and took his pipe out of his mouth to say—'I wouldn't like to be in this ship if ever she heeled to 22 degrees.' 'Don't you think she would come back?' I asked. 'No,' he replied 'I am certain she would capsize.'

He was of course quite wrong, for there were many bouts of much more severe rolling in store for us, and in one storm we achieved a maximum angle of roll of 44 degrees, and this has to be experienced to be believed. To imagine this, think of 45 degrees as halfway between the vertical and the horizontal, so that at 44 degrees the wall, or bulkhead, of the room you are in is to all intents and purposes at the same angle to the vertical as the floor or deck. To move about at this angle, always assuming that the furniture has stayed put, you must have one foot on the bulkhead and one on the deck, and walk along the angle between the two. But of course the furniture does not stay put under these conditions, and long before you reach such an angle it is on the move. It was never anticipated that the *Queen Mary* would roll in this way, and consequently very little of the furniture in the passenger accommodation was rigidly anchored to the floor.

In the large Cabin Class Lounge there was some very expensive and beautiful furniture, heavy settees and easy chairs, large and solidly constructed occasional tables, etc, all of which stood on thick pile carpets, and none of which was anchored to the ship. Under the carpets the floor in this lounge was highly polished, as it was used for dances, and as the rolling increased a critical angle was reached at which the carpets

In mid-Atlantic, looking aft over the stern, the ship beginning to roll. Imagine the tilt to be 44 degrees—no-one took pictures when this angle was reached!

began to slide across the room. This became progressively worse until the whole of the furniture in the room was sliding from side to side, a distance of 70 ft. At the height of the storm in which we rolled to 44 degrees these heavily built settees, which took several men to lift, and the easy chairs and tables, were not merely sliding but rolling over and over from side to side, crashing into the wall at each roll. The crew made valiant attempts to lash some of the furniture to the pillars in the room, but this was a very dangerous exercise and was only partially successful, and for a couple of days and nights the furniture had to be left to its own devices as it was too dangerous to go into the room. The devastation can be imagined.

Conditions in the Tourist and Third Class lounges were just as bad. In one Tourist lounge there was a Challen upright piano in a heavy light oak case, and though this was latched to the bulkhead the screws ultimately pulled out and the piano came free. The result was unbelievable. The room was panelled, and as the piano cannoned its way round—the ship was

pitching as well as rolling—destroying everything in its path, the panelling was ripped to pieces and the wooden case of the piano gradually disintegrated. After two to three days of this the piano was reduced to its iron frame plus strings, and as it cartwheeled round the devastated room it uttered the most weird cacophony of noises.

The plight of the passengers was even worse. Alleyways from cabins to staircases were wide and several hundred feet long. They were smoothly panelled in wood, and there were no handrails, nor anything to hold on to. Once you left your cabin you ricocheted from side to side of the alleyway with no chance of stopping yourself, and many elderly people came to grief this way. If and when you reached the wide open spaces near the stairs you were in worse case, for though the floor was non-slip, the total 'fetch' from one side to the other was about 70 ft, and when the floor was at an angle of over 40 degrees it was impossible to remain standing, and you were just rolled from one side to the other, gathering speed on the way. After the first storm ropes were rigged across all open spaces and this certainly helped, but an indication of the number of accidents caused was the fact that on arrival in Southampton on one trip there were 27 ambulances waiting for us.

This particular storm was classified as a hurricane, and while it was raging no one was allowed out on deck. All the portholes were tightly closed and their dead-lights, which were heavy metal covers, securely fitted. These latter were very necessary and I was once called to a cabin on Main Deck where this had not been done. The pressure of the sea outside burst the ¾ in plate glass of the porthole as though it had been paper, with a report like a cannon going off, and apart from the water that had come in, slivers of glass 3 in-4 in long had travelled horizontally across the cabin and had embedded themselves in the opposite bulkhead. Anyone getting in the way of one of these darts would assuredly have been killed. Even the windows in the Promenade Deck were occasionally burst in this way, and when she was at the end of one of her 44 degree rolls, water was cascading over the Sun Deck, 100 ft from the water line.

In this hurricane, just to add to our discomfort, we answered an SOS, from a steamer called the *Isis*, which was reported to be in a sinking condition several miles south of us. The Captain broadcast an anouncement to the effect that we should be altering course at a certain time and might well heel over as the wind caught us broadside on, but when the time came we were rolling so much that no one noticed any difference.

We received this call for help on Sunday afternoon and arrived at the scene of her last call about 18 hours later. By this time the *Isis* had unfortunately sunk, and together with another ship we searched the area for survivors. In due course a lifeboat was spotted, with one person in it, and some of us rushed up on deck to see it. It was extremely difficult to find it amongst the gigantic waves, as most of the time it was hidden from view, and when I did catch a glimpse of it I was appalled. Until this moment I had not realized just how big the waves were, and the lifeboat was only one tenth of the size of what I had been looking for. How it had ever lived in that welter of white water was a miracle. The *Queen Mary* got to windward of the lifeboat to create a 'lee', and the other ship managed to pick up the lone survivor. We heard later that he was a cabin boy on his first trip to sea.

The effect on passengers of all this movement of the ship in bad weather was dramatic. The crew took it more or less in their stride. After all we were at sea all the time, we were paid to be there, and we had work to do which kept us occupied, and although there were many accidents—one poor stewardess fell down a companionway carrying a tray and was badly injured—and we all got rather tired, life had to go on and the ship had to be run.

But a passenger who was not used to being in a ship, and who, two days after sailing found himself in a situation which appeared to him to be a matter of life and death, became physically and mentally very upset. In bad weather many passengers became seasick, and no doubt they accepted this as part of the price they had to pay. As a storm developed in severity, and the rolling and pitching became worse, mere physical seasickness was overtaken by fear, and under the worst conditions some passengers completely lost their veneer of civilization and became little better than animals.

The Captain was besieged with requests to slow down, to stop, to turn back, to do anything that would lessen the misery, and a rule had to be made that no telephone calls were put through to the bridge. Occasionally some passengers refused to go below in bad storms, and suffered not only from seasickness and fear, but also from cold and wet. They stared at the sea until they became mesmerized by it, and did not really know what was happening. It was by no means a happy sight to see fellow human beings so terrified, and drooling with fear.

Actually there was something definitely hypnotic about the view over the stern of the ship when a big sea was running. The *Queen Mary* was so large, and there was so much ship all around you, that it was quite possible to convince yourself that the ship was standing still, and it was the horizon that was swooping up and down in such an alarming way. I can well believe that if you allowed yourself to be deluded in this way it could be very disturbing.

In calm weather, as you looked over the stern of the ship, the horizon would be level and situated approximately where the rail was. But when the sea was very rough and we were pitching and rolling, the horizon would at one minute be on the left hand side of the stern, up in the air at an angle of 40 degrees or more, and the next moment it would have swooped down out of sight, so that all that could be seen was the sky, and almost immediately it would reappear on the right hand side also up in the air but tilted the other way. And this performance was continuous.

One of the main passenger alleyways, several hundred feet long, and originally with no hand rails nor anything to hold on to (University Archives, University of Liverpool).

Seasickness is a disturbing complaint for which no one as yet seems to have found a complete cure, nor even confidently to have established the cause. One theory is that it is due to upsetting the equilibrium of the fluid in the middle ear, which influences stability and balance. This school of thought claims that anyone who has had scarlet fever is subsequently less prone to seasickness as this disease has the effect of making the inner ear fluid more viscous and less liable to be upset. It is an accepted fact that very young children, and old people, are but slightly affected or escape altogether. It is also maintained that men are not as susceptible as women.

When preparing for a voyage the wisest precautions seem to be to adopt a light diet, to eschew alcohol and tobacco, and to maintain a

Forward funnel and duplicate steam whistles, electrically operated (University Archives, University of Liverpool).

stout heart. Many of our passengers demonstrated that some attacks of seasickness are only in the mind by going down with all the symptoms before the ship had even left the dock!

Speaking personally, I was one of the lucky ones, in that I was never seasick, though prolonged bad weather would sometimes make me dizzy. My immunity I attributed to two incidents early on which boosted my morale. The first of these occurred in our first bad storm when I had to investigate a fault on a lift in the Third Class passenger accommodation. This lift was fairly well forward in the ship, where the motion was much more pronounced, and where your feet felt as if they were leaving the deck when she sank into the trough of a wave. The electrician I was working with, Morton, was very much senior to me, and he stuck me in this lift and made me go up and down in it for some time. The combined motion of the lift and the ship was certainly intriguing but it did not make me feel ill. After a while my colleague left me to finish the job on my own and disappeared, and later that evening he admitted that he had deliberately tried to make me sick. But he was big enough to add that had he not gone to a quieter part of the ship he would have been ill himself.

The second incident occurred the following morning about 5.30 am as I was walking along the Working Alleyway when a passing steward was sick all over my feet, and this did not upset me either. After that, bad weather really had few terrors for me, for which I was devoutly thankful.

Storms in fact had their own excitements and in many ways were exhilarating. The *Queen Mary* had two whistles mounted side by side high up on the forward funnel. They each produced an enormous sound, 'two octaves and two notes below middle C' as the publicity blurb said, and could be heard ten miles away. They were steam whistles, operated by electrical solenoids, and in one gale in the winter I had to go up and change one of the solenoids which was not working.

It was a bitterly cold day, so I put on several sweaters and my patrol jacket underneath my boiler suit—in fact it was difficult to get into the latter. I took the precaution of drawing the fuses for the one whistle that was working, as I did not want anyone pressing the button by mistake while I was up there. The wind was immense up on the funnel and in order to be able to use both hands it was necessary to tie myself on. Apart from being cold it was a magnificent feeling being up there with the wind tearing at you, and in spite of having so much clothing on the wind managed to force my patrol jacket up through the collar of my boiler suit and over my head.

Another fascinating job that came my way in a gale was in the Crow's Nest. This was about 130 ft from the water line and was part of the foremast, being big enough for two people to stand up in. It was reached by climbing up inside the mast, which was hollow, by means of an iron ladder which appeared to go on upwards for ever. The lookout peered over a chin-high parapet, so shaped as to deflect the wind away from him. He had a direct telephone line to the bridge, and an electric radiator to stop him from freezing. His job was to report to the bridge any ship, or other object, that came into view, and woe betide him if the bridge spotted something first.

My job was to repair his radiator, which had ceased to function, and it was in fact the first time I had ever been up in the Crow's Nest. The repair took very little time and I was able to chat for a few minutes with the lookout, who was pleased to have some human company. But the thing that intrigued and delighted me was the very odd sensation of being in the Crow's Nest. From this position you could not see the mast, and so you were unable to see any connection between you and the ship below. You looked down and there she was, a slim elegant ocean greyhound, but you might just as well have been in an aeroplane, completely unconnected.

But the extraordinary sensation occurred when she rolled. When on an even keel the ship was directly below you, but as she rolled she slid away sideways, and at the end of the roll there she was, way out to the left and heeled right over. And while you looked in amazement, quietly and smoothly and before your eyes, she slid sideways underneath you until she was way out to the right. It was the most weird sensation and I could have stayed up there all night watching it.

The reason for the *Queen Mary*'s excessive rolling was soon discovered. She was bottom heavy, rather like those little celluloid dolls of many years ago called 'Kellys', which had a lead weight in their base. You could push them over but they always recovered, swaying backwards and forwards with ever decreasing amplitude until they came to rest. The *Queen Mary* was exactly the same. She had very heavy boilers and engines low down in the ship, and a high superstructure. Her 'wall' was nearly 800 ft long by 135 ft high, and when the wind hit this it pushed her right over. She then sprang back and rolled backwards and forwards in a gradually decreasing arc until the next combination of waves and wind hit her. Her motion was very rapid, and on the top deck you felt you were going to be flung off, like a stone out of a catapult.

The cure was simple in theory—to reduce the metacentric height—but expensive to carry out, and consisted in raising her centre of gravity several inches by putting an additional weight of steel and water ballast fairly high up in the ship. This had a very beneficial effect and we never repeated the rather wild cavortings of that first winter. This was of course before the days of stabilizers, which have now largely removed the problem of rolling from big ships, and hence have contributed much to the peace of mind of passengers.

Though rolling was decidedly uncomfortable and caused many accidents and damage internally in the *Queen Mary*, it was not in itself dangerous, the rough weather that caused it being merely an inconvenience. A much more serious form of bad weather was fog, especially in those pre-war days before radar had been invented.

Above *Foremast and Crow's Nest. Though the picture shows a man apparently climbing an external ladder to the Crow's Nest, this was in fact reached from inside the hollow mast* (University Archives, University of Liverpool).

Left *View of the bow and Crow's Nest from the forward funnel* (University Archives, University of Liverpool).

Our only instrument for detecting the approach of another ship was the human ear, and our only means of knowing we were near an iceberg was the rather strange clamminess in the atmosphere. It was odd too that we could be sailing serenely in the sunshine on an apparently empty sea and then run into a thick bank of fog, and immediately hear numerous ships' whistles around in all directions.

The skipper would slow down in fog, but 80,000 tons moving at 20 knots is for all practical purposes as lethal as at 30 knots, and there were many mixed feelings among the crew as we went belting through the fog with only our whistle blowing a warning.

The lethal properties of the *Queen Mary* were not fully and conclusively demonstrated until 2 October 1943, when she hit the cruiser *Curacao* as she was crossing the *Queen Mary*'s bow. The *Curacao* was acting as escort, and though there was an agreement on the speed to be sailed, she did not really have enough reserve to enable her to zig-zag in front of her charge. The cruiser was hit amidships and cut cleanly in two, each half sinking before it had passed the full length of the *Queen Mary*. Over 300 men were lost in this accident, but down in the *Queen Mary*'s engine room the engineers did not even feel the bump.

To go steaming through fog at high speed therefore, was not felt by some to be quite the thing, and there were two occasions at least in the early days when we were lucky to get away with it. One of these was off the Newfoundland Banks when we actually collided with a small fishing schooner. I was on the 12 to 4 watch, and when I came off at 4 o'clock went straight up on deck to get a breath of fresh air. Almost immediately I heard a banging and shouting on the starboard side, and rushed to look over the side just in time to see this schooner bump her way along our wall, several excited gentlemen on deck swearing at us in French. It was all over in a few seconds and they disappeared into the fog astern. Whether the bridge knew what had happened I never found out.

The second occasion was in European waters, on the trip when we first broke the east to west record. It having been announced that we were going to attempt the record we left Cherbourg at full speed, and in thick fog. Down in the engine room the usual signals were received from the bridge, firstly 'Half Speed Ahead' and then 'Full Speed Ahead'. We then waited for the 'Full Away' signal—which meant that the main steam valves could be tied in the open position, and hopefully left for four days—but instead the

telegraphs clanged 'Stop'. Engineers jumped at the valves to close them, but before they had succeeded in reducing shaft revolutions to any appreciable extent the signal 'Full Speed Astern' came down. At the same instant the ship heeled right over, and we realized that something was wrong, and possibly very wrong.

The *Queen Mary* soon regained an even keel, and in a very short space of time the 'Full Speed Astern' signal was cancelled and we received 'Full Speed Ahead', and then 'Full Away'. Apparently it had been a very close thing, as we had met a German liner, the *Deutschland*, almost head on and travelling at perhaps 19 knots. The heeling over of the ship was due to the avoiding action being taken, and a passenger told me afterwards that he could have shaken hands with those on the deck of the other ship.

There must have been many heart flutterings on the bridge of both ships that day, but we still went ahead at full speed and in fact succeeded in breaking the record. Incidentally, when the signal 'Full Speed Astern' was received from the bridge the shafts were of course turning over in the forward direction, and until they had been stopped it was quite impossible to go full astern by putting astern steam into the turbines. To do so would have ripped out thousands of blades and caused thousands of pounds worth of damage.

Later on, during the war, a friend of mine who was Skipper of a small naval vessel, had the honour of escorting the *Queen Mary* from the Channel up through the Solent to Southampton. Zig-zagging in the approved fashion across the bows of the Queen Mary he kept disappearing from sight from the bridge and, remembering the *Curacao* tragedy, this ultimately preyed on the nerves of the *Queen Mary*'s Captain to such an extent that he flashed a light signal to my friend. It was the single word 'TWERP'. On his next emergence from the shadow of the *Queen Mary*'s bow my friend replied, with the single word— 'TRAMDRIVER!'

Right *Bridge wing and foremast: a view which suggests the height of her 'wall'* (University Archives, University of Liverpool).

Overleaf *The bow, only slightly damaged after sinking HMS* Curacao *during the war, demonstrating both the lethal potential and the strength of the structure* (University Archives, University of Liverpool).

Chapter 13

Bad women (and men)

When the *Queen Mary* was at the height of her popularity an unkind critic described her as a 'floating brothel'. This was very far from the truth, for many thousands of respectable people sailed in her, but there were without question a few of the other sort. Whether the *Queen Mary* had more than other Atlantic liners I would not know, but I can vouch for the fact that generally speaking life aboard this ship was more permissive than ashore.

There were two classes of professionals who 'worked' the Atlantic liners in those days, the courtesans and the con-men, and of the two the former were by far the more interesting. The con-men were mainly card sharpers, but no doubt other activities were practised as well. There are many ways of separating foolish people from their money, and it must be remembered that the *Queen Mary* did inevitably cater for those with more money than discretion.

With this type of passenger about, the *Queen Mary* was a happy hunting ground. The courtesans we carried became well known to us. There were several of them and they would do three or four voyages with us, and then disappear for a similar spell in the *Aquitania*, or the *Normandie*, or the *Bremen*. They were all exceptionally attractive and well groomed women, always travelling First Class, and having apparently an inexhaustible supply of beautiful clothes. The profits they made at this game must have been high, since their overheads were considerable, and it was vital to their success that they should keep up appearances. To my innocent and untutored eye, they were almost indistinguishable from normal lady passengers. I say 'almost indistinguishable', because they were if anything more refined and

presentable. We carried many film stars who earned fabulous salaries, but who were coarse and vulgar in comparison.

One trip when I was working a deck watch, I happened to walk into the main shopping centre on the Promenade Deck about 2 o'clock in the morning to find a fight in progress. This was between two heroes in evening dress who were battling for the favours of one of these elegant creatures. While this was in progress she stood on one side with hand on hip, a picture of frozen loveliness, awaiting the outcome of the contest. The scrap was fairly brisk, there was a little blood and a broken tooth or two, and one of the contestants finally capitulated with a black eye. The victor then dusted himself off, straightened his tie, and he and the prize departed in the direction of the Main Deck cabins. All sterling and stirring stuff, if somewhat primitive, but obviously of a slightly higher class than the fairly common snogging on deck chairs in secluded corners.

Not that all corners were necessarily secluded. The deck chairs supplied by the company were modestly luxurious affairs, solidly constructed and designed for lounging and even for reclining. Some of these were laid out on quite open stretches of deck, but this seemed to make little difference. Indeed in the summer, on hot and humid nights, under almost tropical stars, when the only sounds were the soft whispering of the sea and the breeze gently thrumming in the rigging, the deck chairs were frequently the scene of amorous encounters, and as the night wore on one had to be progressively more broad minded as one walked the deck.

Many were the battles fought on deck chairs in the small hours for the possession of fair ladies,

though it must be said that sometimes the resistance put up was of a token variety, and was perhaps intended mainly to establish her amateur status. One couple, in the heat and excitement of the moment, collapsed their deck chair, but, true to the old showbiz adage, the show went on. Another couple, no doubt in the interests of experimentation, became entangled, not only with each other but with the chair, and had rather ignominiously to be rescued by a steward from what was rapidly becoming a painful and unromantic predicament.

In the lounges too, it was sometimes necessary to look the other way, and on occasion the task of lamping up, which was often our reason for being there in the early hours, became difficult. The presence of electricians however never seemed to deter the combatants, who perhaps felt that our white overalls in some way de-sexed us and rendered us neutral. Or perhaps overalls provided us with a cloak of invisibility, which would at least explain how it came about that we could be completely ignored.

On one occasion I was witness to a romance that went wrong. This was in the Tourist A-Deck Lounge which I entered just as the girl, the injured party, was leaving. She had submitted to, or even assisted in, being undressed, but her friend had obviously gone too far—or perhaps not far enough?—and she had soundly boxed his ear and swept out, naked apart from her shoes and stockings, but proudly and with great dignity clutching her clothes to her bosom.

It was in this same lounge, and indeed on this very settee, that I once saw a girl's legs sticking up into the air over the back. There was no sign of a companion, and as I had no business in going round to the front to see what was going on I never learned the truth, but have often wondered whether perhaps her partner was a contortionist.

One of the many refinements of the *Queen Mary* was the 700-line manual telephone exchange. In the daytime this was manned by three girls, but at night the duty was undertaken by a man. I think it was felt that the girls might be embarrassed in the wee small hours by some of the calls they received, but from my very superficial knowledge of the three ladies concerned I would think the embarrassment might possibly have been on the other side.

When on a 12 midnight to 4.00 am deck watch I used to make it my business to wander into the telephone exchange about 3.00 am as there was

Left *The 700-line telephone exchange* (University Archives, University of Liverpool).

usually a cup of coffee going at the time. On the first occasion when I did this the operator and I sat chatting for some considerable time, with absolutely no activity on the switchboard at all. Then, all of a sudden, dozens of calls started coming through, and the little lights on the switchboard were popping up all over the place. For a few minutes my friend was really busy while I marvelled at this sudden burst of business. When it had died down a bit I asked him what it was all in aid of, and he explained that the Verandah Grill had just closed, and the men had been escorting their new-found girlfriends back to their cabins. Not having the courage to ask outright for an invitation to enter, the men would therefore go back to their own cabins, but would immediately ring their girlfriends up and suggest another, and immediate meeting. A perfectly legitimate use for a telephone exchange, you may say, but not, I imagine, one that the Cunard White Star directors had in mind when they installed it.

On one of my visits to the telephone exchange in the early hours we were joined by the night steward who was on duty on a batch of cabins nearby. He was looking rather down in the mouth and we asked him the reason why. He said he had just been called to a cabin occupied by a single man, who asked him if he drank champagne. He agreed that he did, whereupon the passenger filled his tooth glass from an open bottle and they solemnly had a drink together. The passenger then produced a wad of bank notes and explained that he wanted some female company, and said there was £75 for the woman, and £25 for the steward, if he could find someone suitable.

The steward said he would see what he could do, and departed to think it over. At this point we commiserated with him at not being able to fulfil the order, but he shook his head sadly. 'It's worse than that' he said 'I know of a woman who is available, but she is a bitch, and I am not going to put £75 in her way!'

Much money changed hands in the Cabin Class Smoking Room, but mainly at cards, and on the daily sweepstake. In spite of the published warning about professional gamblers, many men seemed to spend their time playing cards, and stakes were frequently high. On the whole the men who played looked respectable enough, but there were some who looked a little too suave and self-possessed, and whose eyes were cold. No doubt these were actually the good guys and the bad ones were those who looked as if butter would not melt in their mouths. But money was won and lost and there were certainly men who found it a profitable business to travel Cabin Class on the *Queen Mary*. Oddly enough, although the company did warn passengers about them, no warning was issued about the other professionals. Perhaps it was felt that their business was more legitimate, and that at least they were not basically out to cheat their clients.

The daily sweepstake was on the length of the ship's run, and was always conducted in the Smoking Room. The sweep was invariably well patronized, the first prize being £400, which in comparison with the Cabin Class return fare of £110 was a considerable sum of money. This smoking room has been described previously, and its decor was cleverly designed to suggest a high quality, all male, clubroom.

When in New York we had many visitors to the ship, quite a few being Japanese, and we also frequently carried Japanese passengers. The Japs all took a great interest in everything, managed to organize conducted tours of the engine rooms, made copious notes, and made numerous sketches in their little note books, particularly when down below. Several of the engineers felt quite strongly that these visits should be stopped, as the Japs were simply noting design features for use in their own ships at a later date. I did not attach much credence to this until one evening when I had been ashore in New York and returned late to the ship, stopping to chat to the American policeman on duty at the foot of the gangway.

As we were talking a young Japanese came down the gangway and made to walk past us. The policeman, however, held out his hand and stopped him. 'Let me have your camera' he said. Without a word the Japanese fished in an inside pocket and produced a very expensive-looking camera, which the policeman took from him, and equally silently flicked it open, exposed the film that was inside, and handed it back. The Japanese really did have an inscrutable expression on his face as he accepted it, gave the slightest of bows, and walked on.

'How did you know he had a camera?' I asked.

'No Jap goes on a British ship without a camera' the policeman replied. 'I guess they wanna know how you build 'em.' It was not until much later it occurred to me that the Jap was probably clever enough to have changed the film he had shot for a new one beforehand.

This incident reminded me of the story of the Japanese shipping company who ordered two new ships from a Scottish yard. When the first one was delivered and found to be satisfactory,

the Japanese owners sent for the drawings as there were one or two minor alterations they wished to make in the second ship. Once the drawings were in their hands they cancelled the order for this second ship and built it themselves. When they launched her she ran down the ways into the water and promptly capsized, and it transpired that before sending the drawings out to Japan the Scottish firm had subtly altered the design to ensure that this would be so.

The Japanese were not the only visitors we had in New York. Many of the engineers had been sailing into the port for some years, and already had friends in the place. There were also one or two girls who can be best described as 'hangers-on' who were often about, seeking an invitation to stay. Of these girls it was popularly said that they came to have tea and a fight for their honour, but whether the second part of this suggestion had any basis in fact I never found out. Some of these ladies were such tenacious hangers-on that I was always slightly amazed that we managed to get rid of them before we sailed. One girl in particular seemed to turn up every trip, and how she got aboard I do not know, presumably someone must have invited her. On one occasion the engineer she was with was having difficulty in getting her to go, so he craftily introduced her to me and promptly vanished. It was long after the time she should have gone ashore and it took me an acutely embarrassing half hour to persuade her to leave. I was extremely careful on future visits never to renew this particular acquaintance.

Some of the women passengers who did sail from New York in the *Queen Mary* were extremely glamorous. I remember one well-known racing motorist who travelled across several times—each time he had a different girl with him, and each one was more gorgeous than the last one. It was quite a pleasure one day to be asked to connect up his bedside radio, and to see his stunning companion 'in the flesh', as it were. There are some things that money will not buy, but she was definitely not one of them. He was a funny looking fellow, well stepped into middle age, and going thin on top, but he had the charisma of success. I reflected that apart from this I had everything that he had, and what is more I hadn't had it quite so long.

My experience of racing drivers has been very superficial, but it would seem that glamorous women are one of their natural perks. We carried several of them from time to time, and they were all happily accompanied. All but one, that is. This particular man travelled alone and his steward told me that he had the curious habit of saturating six sets of clean towels each day. What he was using them for was never clear.

When on deck watch there were many calls to passengers' cabins to mend lights, or the clock, or telephone, or to put a British type plug on to hair curlers or hair dryers, etc, etc, and one had to learn to be discreet, and not to notice anything out of the ordinary. Passengers were frequently in bed, and I once had to mend a bed reading light while a naked woman lay on the bed covered only with a sheet of newspaper. Presumably she had been reading the newspaper when the light failed! Another time I was asked to repair a light in a bathroom while the girl was in the bath.

These little incidents may not seem very extraordinary now, but in 1936 they were outrageous, and sometimes even the hard-bitten stewards were slightly shocked. For instance, homosexuality was not as acceptable then as it is today, and one steward came into the telephone exchange one night waxing very indignant about the goings-on of two men friends who were sharing a cabin. The steward was not only indignant, but also slightly fearful that he himself might be propositioned.

Two men sharing a cabin was always a dangerous combination, even when their ideas were strictly heterosexual. On one trip from New York two sisters shared a cabin on B-Deck, and as luck would have it there were two men in the adjacent cabin. The men were strangers to each other, and to the two girls, but during the farewell celebrations they got to know each other. We sailed about noon this day, and the quartet had lunch together. After lunch they paired off and went to bed, and there they stayed until Saturday afternoon—three full days—when they appeared briefly, had a quick look round, swapped partners, and went back to bed for the rest of the voyage.

It would not be right to call the *Queen Mary* a floating brothel, but I believe the Greeks would have had a word for it!

Chapter 14

The lighter side

There is an old saying that all work and no play makes Jack a dull boy, and though the 84 engineer officers certainly worked hard, and for long hours, some of us still had the energy and inclination for a bit of leg-pulling. When a bunch of men work together, and live together as well, it is almost inevitable that sooner or later there will be an outbreak of horseplay. In our case this took the form of practical jokes, many of them innocuous, and mostly perpetrated while the recipient was on watch, when it was easy to gain access to his cabin and create havoc.

There were of course all the usual things, such as making 'apple pie' beds, and otherwise interfering with someone's bunk to make it difficult, if not impossible, for him to go to bed. It was a fairly common thing to come off watch and find various lumpy objects, ash trays, hair brushes, books, etc, carefully inserted underneath the bottom sheet, and necessitating the complete remaking of the bed. Pyjamas too had a way of being sabotaged, either tied up in innumerable knots, or stuffed with towels and sheets to form a guy, or even exchanged with those belonging to someone else.

Such tricks were not very original, and not always funny, particularly to the recipient who did not discover the trouble until he was anxious to get into bed. The practical jokers were a comparatively small band of mainly junior engineers, and it was usually possible to hazard a shrewd guess as to who was responsible for a particular outrage. The great thing was to give no visible sign that you had been caught, in the hope that sooner or later the perpetrator would give himself away, which would then open up the road to retribution.

There was a continual search on for original

tricks that had not been used before, many ingenious and even eccentric ideas being put forward. The majority of these did not work, or at best were only partly successful, but there was no doubt that they did liven things up and relieve the monotony of just plugging backwards and forwards across the Atlantic.

One that was worked on one engineer concerned the lights in his cabin. He came off watch one day and switched the light on at the door of his cabin, and nothing happened. Groping around, he tried the reading lamp over the bunk, and that was dead, and so was the one over the wash basin. It seemed logical to assume therefore that a fuse had blown, so he found the fuse box and went through all the fuses. These were all in order, so that he thought perhaps the lamps had gone. But still no luck. This was rather puzzling, and just as he realized that surrounding cabins were not similarly afflicted someone asked him if he was having trouble, and laughed, which gave him the clue that he was being got at.

All that was necessary then was to discover how the lights had been doctored, and this turned out to be a very simple but cunning device. Someone had carefully cut some paper discs and inserted one of these into each bayonet type lamp-holder, so that when the lamp was inserted the two metal contacts on the end were neatly and effectively insulated. The reply to this had to be equally crafty, and after some research work we found out who was responsible and discovered a way of making his lights temporarily inoperable, but we then agreed to call a halt on jokes that interfered with the electricity supply as being too potentially dangerous.

Another joke that was played on me did not have quite the desired effect, and in fact affected me least of all. One day during a spell of rough weather someone shredded up some rubber and mixed it up with the tobacco in my pouch. That night after dinner a number of us were in the wardroom, playing table tennis and reading. I lit my pipe, and before very long the smell was appalling, so bad in fact that the culprit had to admit what he had done, and we ultimately had to evacuate the room and open all the windows.

One trip I managed to put one over on John Rennie. We were both on the same watch, which made it impossible to interfere in any way with his cabin, and he was on duty on the after generating station switchboard, while I was on the forward one. This trip a relief Skipper, Captain Peel, was in charge of the ship, and the weather was pretty hot and sultry. We frequently had Captain Peel with us, and it was an odd thing that his visits always seemed to coincide with a hot and humid spell of weather. So much so in fact that the story got around that he suffered from rheumatism, and deliberately took a more southerly course in order to get into the warmer weather. For this reason he was not popular in the engine room, where it was already uncomfortably hot.

On this particular trip we left New York, where the weather is impossibly humid in the summer, and seemed to shoot off south down to the tropics, since the weather, if anything, got warmer and stickier. So, in the middle of one watch, I rang up John Rennie on his switchboard, disguised my voice as best I could, and we had a conversation that went something like this:

'This is the navigating bridge speaking.'

'Oh yes' said John, immensely flattered to think that the bridge were calling him.

'May I speak to Mr Rennie?'

'This is Mr Rennie speaking.'

'We are getting up a small testimonial fund for Captain Peel, as a mark of our respect and esteem, and we wondered if you would care to contribute?'

'Yes, indeed' said John, 'I should be happy to.'

'It is quite a small fund, but we wish to buy him a suitable present, to be given to him from a few of his personal friends among the officers.'

Still John did not smell a rat, and in fact swallowed the bait with one gulp.

'What form is the present to take?.

'We are thinking of buying him a pair of Bermuda shorts, because if the bastard takes us any further south he is certainly going to need them!'

There was a long pause, and then suddenly the penny dropped, and he realized that his leg was being pulled.

'You blankety-blank-blank-blank!' I heard him say as I put the phone down and hurried down the ladder to the turbine floor below.

Within a few seconds the phone rang, and I had to climb the ladder up to the switchboard to answer it. It was John.

'Did you just ring me up?' he demanded.

'Me?' I said. 'I've just been down on the turbines.' Which was nothing but the truth, if not the whole truth. So he told me what had happened, still not realizing who had fooled him. But he guessed when he asked me if I had been similarly approached and I told him no, I was not a *personal* friend of Captain Peel's!

John came in for more ragging one day when he was cleaning out his goldfish tank. Perhaps I should explain that one of the 'cargoes' carried by the *Queen Mary* from America to England were goldfish from Japan, consigned to Woolworths. For these we had a special tank on D-Deck which measured perhaps six feet long by two feet wide and four feet deep, and this was crammed with fish until they were literally almost a solid mass, and were quite unable to swim about. To keep them alive air had to be pumped in at a prodigious rate, and even then mortality was high, and on one dreadful occasion when the pump failed the whole lot died, within minutes, and had to be shovelled out.

Under these conditions it was a humanitarian gesture to take out a few fish and give them a slightly better life, and there was absolutely no question of any being missed. Consequently, in the fullness of time, every engineer officer had his own little aquarium containing a few fish, and these provided a constant source of interest. Without being in any way expert we tended to vie with each other and boast about our favourite fantail, or shubunkin, or whatever.

One morning John Rennie was cleaning out his aquarium in the presence of one or two of his friends, who were watching the operation keenly and looking out for an opportunity of playing some sort of trick on him. To the best of my recollection he had only three or four fish, quite small ones, but they included one of which he was particularly fond on account of its delicate shape and glorious colour. He decanted the fish into his wash basin and turned his attention to cleaning out the actual tank. This took a little time and when it was ready it had to be filled with clean water. While his attention was distracted, Jock Baxter—who was usually involved when some devilment was about—managed to transfer the fish from the wash basin to another receptacle, and just as John turned to the wash basin to

get the fish we pulled out the plug and let out all the water. The timing could not have been better, for John saw the last of the water going out and was convinced that the fish had gone out with it.

For a few moments he was furious, but his delight on having his fish restored to him safe and sound was beautiful to behold, though for a long time he was muttering dark threats of reprisals. Actually the goldfish in engineers' cabins, though undoubtedly having a better life style than those in the bulk tank down below, led a somewhat perilous existence particularly when the ship was rolling badly. One engineer, who omitted to secure his aquarium to the bulkhead, did in fact lose his fish, finding their little bodies scattered round the cabin when he came off watch, together with a couple of gallons of water and associated weed and gravel.

Off watch there were many opportunities for wandering round the ship, particularly in the 'unsocial hours' when there were no passengers about, and one of my favourite pastimes was to play the piano. There were several pianos in the ship, all different, but all beautiful instruments, my favourite being a Chappell grand in the Studio. This room was in the Cabin Class accommodation, and was provided for the benefit of passengers who were professional performers, and wished to practice during the voyage. The Studio was sound proofed so that it was possible to go in and play the piano there without being a nuisance to anyone.

Another diversion, which would never have been officially condoned, and which could therefore only be indulged in the early hours of the morning, was to steer the ship. The *Queen Mary*'s steering engine was a massive piece of machinery, but her wheel was smaller than in many yachts, and was so light that it could easily be moved with one finger. Very often, during the small hours when the Officer of the Watch was somewhere else, the bridge would be untenanted except for the quartermaster who was steering. If the weather was fair, and he was feeling friendly, or wanted to disappear for a moment for a quick smoke, he would surrender the wheel and leave you to it. Steering this great ship was very simple. Immediately above the wheel were two instruments, a course indicator, which showed

you the compass course you were on, and a rudder indicator, which showed the angle the rudder was making with the ship. With one finger it was possible to keep her on course, or to steer her round in a great circle.

There was something uncanny, and not a little thrilling, about standing there alone in the dark on this huge bridge, knowing that you were, however superficially, controlling a multi-million pound ship, and that there were upwards of 3,000 people completely dependent upon you. It brought home the fearful responsibility that rested on the Captain, week in and week out, in fair weather or foul, of bringing this ship safely across the Atlantic.

'The Blue Riband of the Atlantic', the coveted title bestowed on the ship holding the record for a crossing, was really a bit of a joke, or at best a publicity gimmick. It was believed that to be able to claim to be the fastest ship on the North Atlantic attracted customers, and this may well have been the case, but in 1936 there was so little to choose in speed between the *Queen Mary* and the *Normandie* that it really lost a lot of its meaning. We firmly believed that the *Queen Mary* was the better ship, and liked to think of the *Normandie* having to slow down so that the passengers could eat, but there was no doubt they were both very fast.

I have mentioned in Chapter 7 that it was decided not to break the record on the maiden voyage but to wait a while until more publicity was required. This moment arrived in July, and on the voyage commencing Wednesday 22 July 1936 the *Queen Mary* was instructed by Head Office to break the East to West record—by four hours. Note that this decision was taken by Liverpool and that the time by which the record had to be lowered was specified, for in the event we arrived at the other side too soon, and had to slow down.

There was a great upsurge of interest when the *Queen Mary* broke the record, her time on this occasion for a passage of 3,098 nautical miles being 4 days, 8 hours, and 37 minutes, corresponding to a speed of 29.61 knots. On the Saturday of this voyage she covered 760 miles, her speed for this day being almost 31.7 knots.

This record was held for a few months until the *Normandie* recaptured it, and so it went on, in both directions, each ship monotonously breaking the record, until no one really knew or cared very much as to who held what. But one thing the Blue Riband did do; it focused attention on the *Queen Mary* and *Normandie*, and away from the *Bremen* and *Europa*.

Left *John Rennie and author. Self-taken picture by lashing the camera to the rail and operating the trigger with a length of cotton. Whose hand held the cotton?* (C. W. R. Winter collection).

The two German ships were very smart and very efficient motor ships, but just a little slower than the *Queen Mary*. We had many friendly and unofficial races across the Atlantic with them, races which they were inevitably destined to lose. The *Bremen* and *Europa* ran a regular service into New York and docked at a pier just below ours. Whichever one of them was in New York when we were, usually left for Europe about twelve hours before us, her first port of call being the same as ours, namely Cherbourg. Her departure would be quite spectacular, with the band playing on deck, and streamers and bunting everywhere. If it was after dark, the Nazi flag at the gaff of her main-mast would be floodlit.

In contrast, our departure twelve hours later would be a very dull affair, as we slipped out without any fuss or bother. Then, 36 hours out, we would catch up the German ship, and as soon as we spotted her hull down on the horizon she would see us too, and great volumes of black smoke would issue out of her funnels. We used to say in fun that her Skipper was burning the furniture in an attempt to get away from us, but it was no use, we were faster than she was, and slowly but surely overhauled her, very often passing quite close, which seemed to be rubbing her nose in it a bit.

On one eastward voyage we did not catch the German until we reached Cherbourg, where she dutifully stopped to pick up a pilot. Our Captain seized this golden opportunity and steamed straight into the harbour unaided, and as there was only one berth which we both used, the other ship had to wait outside until we came out.

We were very pleased with our Skipper that day for, had we had to wait outside while the German ship unloaded her passengers, we would have lost the tide up Southampton Water and been late home. Calling at Cherbourg on the homeward run was always a major irritation with the crew, all of whom were eager to get home. What added to the irritation was that in New York there was always plenty of time to spare.

One diversion that occasionally passed the time in New York was boat drill, and in the summer this was a pleasant exercise. The passengers had a kind of boat drill on every voyage, this being little more than mustering at their boat station with their life jacket, and being taught how to put it on. But at least they did know how to find their own particular lifeboat in the event of an emergency.

For the crew however boat drill was rather different. To begin with drills were only held infrequently, the most important aspect of them being to check that the boats and launching mechanisms were working properly. Each boat was designed to carry 144 persons, including a specified number of engineers, and it was our job to see not only that the boat winches were in working order, but also that the boat engines could be started easily. Every boat from time to time was lowered into the water, and in the hot weather it was very pleasant to chug up and down the Hudson River for a short spell. It was obviously very important that these mechanical checks should be carried out, so that in the event of an emergency as few mistakes as possible should be made. Even in a ship as well run as the *Queen Mary* mishaps did occur, as the following anecdote will illustrate.

When we reached the Ambrose Light Vessel on the way out from New York the engines were temporarily stopped while we dropped the pilot, and then it was full speed ahead for home. As more steam was fed into the main propulsion turbines and the ship rapidly gathered speed we were busy down below since all the auxiliaries had to be speeded up, and the electrical load climbed quickly. It was necessary to anticipate this rapid increase by starting up another turbo-generator, and for a time this spare machine was running light, that is, carrying no load.

On one such occasion the Staff Chief Engineer, who ought to have known better, saw on his monitor instrument on the forward engine room starting platform that one of the turbo-generators was carrying no load, so he rang through on the generator room telegraph to shut it down. The engineer on watch was in rather a quandary. He knew that in a very short time this generator was going to be needed, so he phoned the engine room for confirmation of the order—and got it, in explicit terms. So he shut the machine down.

Almost immediately after this the load began to rise, until the two generators which were running became overloaded. Then things began to happen. As a safeguard there were certain circuits which were arranged to trip out in the event of overload, and these trips now came into operation. Unfortunately these had never been checked or it would have been realized that one of these circuits fed the boiler feed pumps. So a chain reaction started. As the supply of water to the boilers dropped, so the steam pressure dropped, and as this happened so, of course, the turbo-generators slowed down and the voltage dropped. This caused more circuits to trip out, all the lights in the passenger accommodation went out, the ship came to a standstill, and for a time down below all was confusion and chaos. Fortunately a complete shutdown was avoided, but we got down to a situation where there was only enough steam to run one generator. From this one machine however we managed to get the boiler feed pumps running again, and gradually the main boilers got back into business and the load was carefully and laboriously built up again.

Whether the Staff Chief Engineer ever got into trouble for this rather elementary mistake the junior engineer officers never knew, but the incident caused us all a lot of amusement as he was very full of his own importance, and was not very popular. I would dearly have loved to hear the subsequent conversation between the little bumptious Yorkshireman, Sutcliffe the Staff, and the equally fiery Welshman, Roberts the Chief.

Chapter 15

Memories

One of the most marvellous things about the human memory is that it tends to discard the unpleasant and uncomfortable, and retain only the enjoyable images, so that a sailor forgets the long and tiring hours, and the frequent beastliness of the weather when it was impossible to sleep. Instead one remembers the blissful days when the sun shone and the sky was blue, and the colour of the sea was such a dark, dark blue as to be almost black. One remembers warm moonlit nights, and the incredible colours flecking the pure whiteness of the bow wave when the morning sun first broke the horizon. One remembers too the sounds made by a great ship as she sped serenely through the sea, the distant hum of machinery, the noise of the quarter wave as it fled away from the ship, the occasional tremble of vibration as the ship dipped gracefully to the sea.

Against this background other memories of events connected with the ship stand out clearly and sharply, never to be completely erased. For example, no one who sailed in the *Queen Mary* on her maiden voyage would ever forget the tumultuous welcome that awaited us in New York. Conversely, neither would one ever entirely expunge the memory of the mammoth seas we met in the winter of 1936, with the ship rolling to over 40 degrees so that the waves were lapping over the Sun Deck which was normally a hundred feet from the water level.

Although in her first years of service she did not visit many different places there are also memories of beautiful spring days in Scottish waters, and of seeing the mountains of Mourne rise out of the sea. As a member of the crew one naturally remembers the comradeship of one's fellow engineers, and the fun that was had, just as

one remembers the thrill each and every day of stepping out on deck and seeing the apparently limitless ocean stretching away to the horizon.

And I shall never forget, at the end of my soujurn in her, the queer little feeling of desolation and despair on seeing the ship—my ship—sail away without me.

Fortunately however, most memories are pleasant ones, and many are connected with the passengers who travelled with us. One trip in summer we carried a bunch of American students off on a tour of Europe. The nights were warm and still, and after dinner they congregated on deck and sang student songs. I shall never hear *Santa Lucia* again without remembering the sighing of the warm summer breeze in the rigging, and the lazy way the stars swung back and forth as the ship moved to the sea.

Another memory which still haunts me, again on deck and at night, is of a west-bound trip in, I think, 1937, just after the 'Anschluss' in Austria when Hitler invaded that beautiful but defenceless country and drove out thousands of its nationals. Many hundreds of them crossed the Atlantic to seek safety in America, and sad indeed was their plight. The majority had been forced to leave everything behind, so sudden had been their departure, and had it not been for the welfare organizations who cared for them many would have starved. Where the money came from I do not know, but the Cunard White Star Company issued vouchers to them which they could spend aboard, and generally did everything possible to alleviate their distress. They travelled Third Class, and a pathetic group of people they were, drawn from all walks of life, all suffering from bewilderment and shock at the sudden upheaval which had thrown them out of their homes, all worried and anxious at the prospect of having to build an entirely new life in the New World.

At Sun Deck level it was possible to walk round in front of and below the bridge and look down on the Third Class deck in the bow of the ship. One dark night after dinner I happened to walk this way, and shall never forget the experience. The deck below was dark and there was no movement, but here and there a cigarette glowed and one could sense the presence of many people. The ship lifted easily to the swell, and down there among the shadows someone was playing a violin, sad little gypsy melodies that contained all the sadness and pathos in the world. No one spoke or moved, and the unseen violinist played on and on, expressing far more eloquently and movingly the tragedy that had overcome their homes and country, and which was about to engulf the whole of the western world.

Another memory, of a very different kind, is of the American Legion which was holding a mammoth convention in New York one week when we were there. The American Legion is a parallel organization to our own British Legion, with similar aims and objects, but in character they could not be more different. Once every year or so the Legion staged a convention in some large American city, and this was attended by thousands of their World War I ex-service members. At the end of the convention they transferred *en masse* to Europe for a tour of the battlefields, travelling in the grand manner by chartering their own ship, which for the purpose of the trip they re-named '*The Mayflower*'. I suppose in 1937 the average age of the Legionnaires must have been about 50, but their exuberance knew no bounds, and they were more lively than any bunch of schoolboys could possibly have been.

Every town and city in the States sent a contingent to this convention, some of them quite large, and each contingent was dressed in its own design of uniform. There may be those who think that the official American Army and Air Force uniforms are a little ornate, with too many fancy badges and medal ribbons, but these uniforms are drab and dull compared to the outfits displayed by the Legion. A Ruritanian musical comedy chorus boy would look sombre and sad against the average legionnaire.

Many of the larger contingents also had their own military band, and these were generally of a very high standard. Every band had its own bevy of gorgeous drum-majorettes, and these were not only attractive to look at, but were extremely efficient at their job. Bands were continually parading up and down Broadway and neighbouring streets, and normal traffic requirements took a very back seat.

Another disruptive influence was the number of unusual vehicles brought by the legionnaires, many of these resembling carnival floats, and it appeared that the larger contingents vied with each other in producing outlandish designs. One group of warriors rode round in a train consisting of an engine and three coaches. The engine was obviously built on the chassis of a lorry, but it made the right noises for a locomotive, and real steam puffed out of its funnel. Another group had a large open motor car which looked normal enough until it stopped at a traffic light, when it slowly tipped up on its back wheels until it was vertical instead of horizontal, its four occupants sitting motionless the while. When the light turned green it slowly resumed a horizontal position and proceeded on its way as though nothing had happened.

Legionnaires on foot were also busy adding gaiety to the town. In Times Square there was a single-storey newspaper and magazine kiosk which had a flat roof, and two legionnaires occupied this roof. One sat on a little camp stool while the other knelt in front of him with a basin of water. He carefully and slowly removed one of his friend's shoes and sock, washed his foot in the basin and then subjected it to a careful examination, shaking his head slowly and sorrowfully. He then put the shoe and sock back on again, and proceeded to do the same thing with the other foot. This process apparently went on indefinitely, for an hour later they were still there, being watched intently by a crowd of several hundreds.

At night things hotted up and some of their tricks verged on the dangerous, as for example the grand piano which they dropped from a high floor of a 42nd Street hotel on to the pavement below. They took the precaution of clearing quite a large area of the street beforehand, and no one appeared to get hurt. The police took a benevolent view of all these proceedings, and in fact kept discreetly out of the way. They were not present at the piano dropping exploit, and the only policemen I saw that night were riding glumly on the roof of a single-deck trolley-car.

When we sailed from New York to return to Europe we carried a few hundred legionnaires who had not been able to secure berths on their chartered ship, and they must have found their surroundings a bit tame in comparison. They quite seriously wished to take over control of the *Queen Mary*, and were rather surprised and disappointed when they were not even allowed up on the bridge. Though the Captain was unsympathetic to their requirements the crew responded with alacrity to the situation and set up, in the tween-decks, a school of 'Housey-housey' which ran non-stop, 24 hours a day, until the last legionnaire had left the ship in Cherbourg. The pickings were rich, and to parody a once famous saying, never in the history of human transport was so much taken off so many by so few.

But my fondest memories of my time in the *Queen Mary* will always be connected with the reactions of American passengers to their arrival in the English Channel. Even seasoned travellers never failed to remark on how green the country looked from the sea, and this was in startling contrast to the coastline of America which invariably appeared drab and brown. England truly is a green and pleasant land.

Usually, however, our first intimation that we were approaching land came on the Sunday evening, often in the dark, and it was a strange fact that the reaction of American passengers on reaching the Channel was totally different from their reaction on arriving back in America. There was much more of a feeling of homecoming on reaching Europe, and I suppose this may have been due to the fact that their ancestors were in all probability European.

I shall long remember one particular occasion when I was walking up the ship's main com-panionway after the news had gone round that land had been sighted. An American girl ran past me up the stairs to join her mother who was a few steps ahead. I never saw her face, and only had the merest glimpse of a dark curly head peeping out of a large fur-collared overcoat before she was gone again, but I heard her voice, and I heard what she said. It was quite simple really—she just said 'Oh, there's *land*!'

Print cannot convey one hundredth part of the passionate excitement she got into those three words, nor can it describe the unexpected thrill of homecoming that I experienced. I went out on to the dark deck, and there sure enough was the Bishop Light winking away, saying 'Here you are, here you are, not far to go now!' And a little further on, ahead of the ship, was the slow and steady alternate red and white glow of the Wolf Rock Light saying—

'Steady on now, there's no need to hurry. This is England all right.'

While over the horizon came the loom of the Lizard's quick, nervous flash, which seemed to say—

'Oh do buck up, please. Don't keep me standing here all night!'

If she had only known it, that American girl was but echoing the thoughts of countless thousands of seafarers throughout the centuries on making their landfall, and just for a moment I shared all her excitement. As I stood out there under the stars I experienced a great wave of pride and humility; pride in my country, pride in my ship, and humility that I was fortunate enough to be a part of both.

Index